A DICTIONARY OF BRITISH STUDIO POTTERS

A Dictionary of
British Studio Potters

Pat Carter

Scolar Press

© Pat Carter 1990

Published by
SCOLAR PRESS
Gower Publishing Company Limited
Gower House
Croft Road
Aldershot
Hants GU11 3HR
England

Gower Publishing Company
Old Post Road
Brookfield
Vermont 05036
USA

British Library Cataloguing in Publication Data
Carter, Pat
    A dictionary of British studio potters.
    1. British pottery
    I. Title
    738.3'0941

ISBN 0-85967-800-8

Printed in Great Britian by
Thomson Litho Ltd, East Kilbride, Scotland

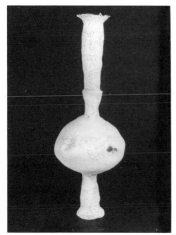
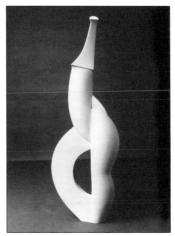

Contents

Preface

In writing this Dictionary, I have attempted to collect together the names of those people who have been working in Britain this century as studio potters. Many are well known, others less so, but I hope that this will provide a comprehensive guide to both new collectors and old enthusiasts.

One or two potters have asked that their names be excluded, and I have respected their wishes.

My thanks go to all those potters who have so willingly assisted me, and to the photographers sadly too numerous to mention. Especial thanks to Cyril Frankel of Bonhams, Paul Greenhalgh of Christie's, Barley Roscoe of the Crafts Study Centre, Bath, Marta Donaghey of the Craftsmen Potters Association, and to Shelagh Flack.

Pat Carter
October 1989

Note from the publisher

Wherever possible, an example of each potter's work and mark is reproduced. The word 'signature' indicates that the potter's mark takes the form of his or her signature.

Nancy Angus

Born in 1958 in Bath. Now lives in Brighton. Studied ceramics at Bath Academy of Art and South Glamorgan Institute of Higher Education. In 1982 she became resident artist at Crewe and Alsager College and stayed on to teach part time on the Crafts course. She moved to Brighton in 1985, joining the newly established Red Herring Studios. She is a part time lecturer at Portsmouth College of Art, Design and FE.

Her pots and dishes are hand-built and decorated with coloured slips and underglaze or bodystains before firing. Nancy Angus uses a wide range of decorative techniques including paper stencils, plaster and sponge, stamps, and sgraffito.

Major exhibitions inlude: Jugend Gestaltet, Munich; Fitzwilliam Museum, Cambridge; Galerie L. Hamburg; Design Centre and Craft Gallery, Leeds; Nexus, Brighton; Contemporary Applied Arts; Craft & Folk Museum, Los Angeles; Courcoux and Courcoux, Salisbury; Primavera, Cambridge.

Work included in a number of public collections.

Dan Arbeid

Born in London in 1928, he left school at fourteen and worked in tailoring until 1955. The following year he began work in a ceramics factory in Israel. This inspired him to return to England to attend the Central School of Art, and he began to concentrate on hand built stoneware. Much of his early work was made at the Abbey Art Centre, New Barnet. He moved to Essex, setting up a workshop in a converted victorian school. His work, individual large pieces in stoneware, emphasizes the different techniques of hand built pottery – wheel made, coiled, beaten and folded, thrown and turned. Considerable teaching duties at Camberwell and the Central School have limited his output over the years.

Major exhibitions include: Primavera London and Cambridge from 1959; British Crafts Centre, London; Craftsmen Potters Association; School of Applied Art, Bristol; Molton Gallery, London; Boymans Museum, Rotterdam; National Museum of Wales; Kestner Museum, Hanover; Prague, Tokyo and Oslo.

Work represented in public collections in many countries.

Paul Astbury

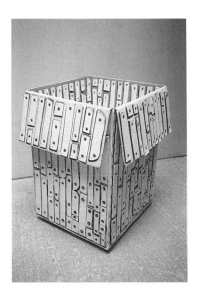

Born in 1945 in Cheshire. Lives in London. Studied painting, sculpture and ceramics at Stoke on Trent, then ceramics at the Royal College of Art under Hans Coper and Eduardo Paolozzi. The influences on his work have been varied – from occult imagery and science fiction to particle physics. The major theme of his work is the fragmentation of form and surface.

Lectures at Middlesex Polytechnic and South Glamorgan Institute of Higher Education.

He uses porcelain, press moulding and slabbing, working on the surface with inks, oxides, oil, adhesives, etc. The pieces are unglazed and fired to 1260°C. He is developing his theme of fragmentation of surface through painting and ceramics, finding strong relationships between the two.

Major exhibitions include: Everson Museum of Art, New York; British Council exhibition to Australia and New Zealand; British Crafts Centre; Yorkshire Sculpture Park; Aberystwyth Arts Centre, Wales; Manchester City Art Gallery.

Ian Auld

Born in 1928 in Brighton. Studied painting at Brighton at the Slade before turning to pottery. He spent three years in the Middle East establishing a pottery department at Baghdad and returned to Essex where he began to make slab built stoneware decorated with seals, impressed and incised patterns. He taught at the Central School and Camberwell, then succeeded James Tower in 1965 as senior lecturer at Bath Academy of Art, later moving to Bristol Polytechnic. In 1970 he undertook a research fellowship in Nigeria, and on returning took up appointment as Head of Ceramics at Camberwell. He is no longer potting. His work is architectural and sculptural rather than functional, sometimes just a simple shape such as a cube or rectangle.

Major exhibitions include: Primavera, London; Crafts Centre, London; Craft Centre, Copenhagen; Craftsmen Potters Association, London; Boymans Museum, Rotterdam; Exposition Nationale, Geneva; Japan, Italy, France and Germany.

Work represented in many public collections in UK and overseas.

Felicity Aylieff

Born in 1954 in Bedfordshire. Lives in Bath. Trained at Bath Academy of Art and Goldsmiths' College, London. On leaving Goldsmiths she taught pottery and art at Bedales School for three years. She now teaches at Bath and Goldsmiths'. The influence for her pottery comes from Egyptian, African and South American Art, with decoration derived from Japanese, Chinese, Indian, Greek and Islamic patterns. Colour is of great importance.

Felicity Aylieff's pots are handbuilt, slabbed or coiled using white earthenware. Sometimes the clay is stained, sometimes made plain. It is then inlaid with mixed coloured clay shapes. The pots are once fired at 1220°C and polished to a smooth finish. Glaze is rarely used.

Major exhibitions include: Amalgam, Barnes; Beaux Arts, Bath; Contemporary Applied Arts; New Ashgate Gallery, Farnham; Open Eye Gallery, Edinburgh; Oxford Gallery; St James' Gallery, Bath; Terrace Gallery, Worthing; Westminster Gallery, Boston; Hannah Peschar Gallery, Ockley.

Gordon Baldwin

Born in 1932 in Lincoln. Lives in Berkshire. Studied at Lincoln School of Art and the Central School of Art and Design, in Painting and Drawing and Industrial as well as Studio Pottery. He has taught pottery at Eton College since 1957. He is a sculptor and a painter who uses ceramic materials as his medium. Large coiled bowls are one of his major forms.

Gordon Baldwin uses buff clay worked on with layer on layer of thin white slip or engobe. On top of the slips are painted and drawn designs with incised lines and on glaze stains. Each piece is subject to numerous firings.

Major exhibitions include: Seibu Gallery, Tokyo; Contemporary Applied Arts; Crafts Council, Victoria and Albert Museum, London; Pennsylvania State University; Cleveland County Museum; Schneider Gallery, West Germany; Solomon Gallery, London; Palazzo Agostinelli, Bassano, Italy; International Art Fair, Chicago; Fitzwilliam Museum, Cambridge.

Work represented in many public collections in UK and overseas.

Alan Barrett-Danes

Born in 1936 in Kent. Now living in Wales. Trained with his grandfather at the Upchurch Pottery in Kent and at Maidstone and Stoke-on-Trent Colleges of Art. After twelve years designing for the pottery industry he began teaching and is now senior lecturer at the Institute of Higher Education, South Glamorgan. From years of working in collaboration with Ruth his wife, he has returned to exploring wheel thrown forms. He works in many different clays fired to 1000°–1500°C. His series of jug forms range from Russian inspired ritualistic urns to the latest bird-based vessels.

Major exhibitions include: Galerie L, Hamburg; Welsh Crafts Touring Exhibition; Copernican Connection, Beverley; Chepstow Gallery, Gwent; Craftsmen Potters Association.

Ruth Barrett-Danes

Born in 1940 in Plymouth. Now lives in Wales. Studied at Plymouth and Brighton Colleges of Art. Undertakes some part-time teaching at the University Hospital of Wales.

Ruth Barrett-Danes makes individual figurative pieces in porcelain, some based around a vessel form. They have visual and literary influences, from early Celtic Art to Breughel and Rodin, from Gilgamesh to Blake and Ted Hughes. They are handbuilt by pinching, coiling, slabbing, modelling and carving. The work has evolved from one simple dominant form in conflict with the predatory creature to larger vessels where the inhabitants are absorbed into the structure. Recent work has dispensed with the underlying forms.

Major exhibitions include: Westminster Gallery, Boston; Oxford Gallery; British Craft Centre/Contemporary Applied Arts; Charlotte Hennig, Darmstadt; Beaux Arts, Bath; Keramik Galerie Böwig, Hannover; Copernican Connection, Beverley; Craftsmen Potters Association.

Paul Barron

1917–1983. Studied pottery at Brighton School of Art under Norah Braden and at the Royal College of Art with Helen Pincombe. With Henry Hammond he helped to build up the Ceramics Department at Farnham School of Art. In 1953 he established a studio at nearby Bentley which he shared with Henry Hammond until his death.

He worked in stoneware making wheel thrown individual pieces and some domestic ware. Wood ash glazes were an important feature of his work.

Major exhibitions include: New Ashgate Gallery, Farnham; Guildford House, Guildford; Craftsmen Potters Association; Takashimaya Store, Tokyo; Amsterdam, Prague.

Work represented in a number of UK public collections including the Victoria and Albert Museum.

Svend Bayer

Born in 1946 in Uganda. Now lives in Devon. Trained at Wenford Bridge Pottery as a pupil of Michael Cardew between 1969 and 1972, then worked for a year as a thrower at Brannam's Pottery, Barnstaple. After visiting potteries in Japan, Korea and South East Asia, and setting up a pottery in Connecticut, he established his own pottery in Devon where he uses local clay and a woodfired kiln, fired to 1320°C to produce a range of domestic and garden pots. The major influences on his work have been Michael Cardew, North Devon Slipware, Chinese, Korean and Thai stoneware. All his work is thrown on a kick wheel. Some is glazed and decorated, but mostly rely on the woodfiring for the finished appearance.

Major exhibitions include: Amalgam, London; North Cornwall Museum and Gallery; Crafts Study Centre, Bath; Contemporary Applied Arts; Sultan Gallery, Kuwait; Alder Biesen, Belgium; Craftsmen Potters Association.

Michael Bayley

MB

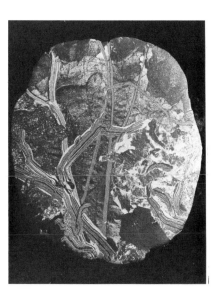

Born in 1932 in Kimbolton. Lives in Kent. Trained at Hornsey College of Art in the 1950s, and opened his present workshop in Dover while teaching part time in a local school. This he continues to do. He is influenced by forms and rhythms in the natural world-landscape, rocks, the seashore. His pots are hand-built from stoneware and porcelain and textures and patterns are made by rolling coloured clays into one another. Striped patterns are formed by laminating different clays, and slicing through them. His pieces are once fired at 1260–1280°C and mostly unglazed. His recent work tends towards a brighter range of colours, rougher edges, and greater assymetry.

Major exhibitions include: Craftsmen Potters Association; Contemporary Ceramics from Europe, Stuttgart; Mid Cornwall Galleries; European Potters, Darmstadt.

Work represented in public collections in Europe, USA and Japan.

Peter Beard

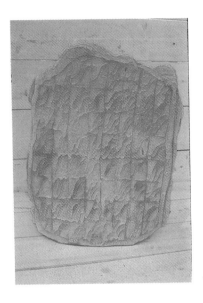

Born in Southport, Lancashire in 1951. Started working in potteries in 1965 which fired his interest in ceramics. he studied industrial and furniture design at Ravensbourne College of Art. On completion of his course in 1973 he moved to Scotland to help set up a pottery making domestic ware. He first opened a studio in Kent in 1975 making one-off pieces and sculpture. He teaches part time at Kent Institute for Art and Design.

His current work is mostly stoneware, thrown and handbuilt with some modelled additions and with matt and semi-matt glazes in pastel shades used in layers to create coloured textures and patterns.

Major exhibitions include: Peter Dingley, Stratford-upon-Avon; Rye City Art Gallery; Galerie An Gross St Martin, Cologne; Liberty, London; Innate Harmony, London; Craftsmen Potters Association.

Dora Billington

No mark used

1890–1968. Born in Stoke on Trent, she studied at the Henley School of Art and the Royal College of Art where she taught ceramics for a while. In 1924 she took charge of the pottery class at the Central School of Arts and Crafts, when it was little more than a pottery painting class. Because of her drive and energy, and her sound knowledge and understanding of techniques and materials, the class developed into a department of serious study and achievement.

She exhibited her work with the Arts and Crafts Exhibition Society.

Sebastian Blackie

Born in 1949 in Huntingdonshire. Now lives in Surrey. Trained at Cambridge College of Art, Farnham School of Art and Goldsmiths' College, London. Studied ceramics under Henry Hammond and Paul Barron. Began teaching part time in 1973, and in 1982 became Head of the School of Ceramics at West Surrey College of Art and Design, Farnham. Continues to exhibit regularly despite this commitment, together with part time teaching overseas.

He works in stoneware, coiling and adding layers of minerals to the dry clay which is then fired repeatedly, developing surfaces integrated with, and peculiar to each form. A range of kilns are used, including one constructed from paper, of prehistoric design.

Major exhibitions include: Leeds City Art Gallery; Scottish Gallery; Oxford Gallery; Gallery Siders, Norway; Amalgam, Barnes; Anatol Orient, London; Craftsmen Potters Association.

Betty Blandino

Born in London and now lives in Oxford. Studied painting at Goldsmiths' College, and pottery with Gordon Baldwin and Ian Auld. Betty Blandino, a former teacher and director of the Upper Gallery in Whitechapel, has been making stoneware pots since 1973. They are hand-built by coiling and pinching, decorated by means of dry-brushing oxides and slip over certain areas, and fired to 1260°C. Her work is becoming more asymmetrical and sculptural, the movement and balance of the piece being of prime importance.

Major exhibitions include: Peter Dingley, Stratford-upon-Avon; Beaux Arts, Bath; Oxford Gallery; Primavera, Cambridge; Galerie Somers, Heidelberg; Galerie L, Hamburg; New College, Oxford.

Work represented in many museums and public collections in UK and overseas.

Katharine Pleydell Bouverie
'Beano'

1895–1985. Began her pottery training at the Central School of Arts and Crafts under Dora Billington. She joined the Leach Pottery as one of Bernard's earliest pupils in 1924. A year later she returned home to Coleshill, Wiltshire, to set up a pottery with Ada Mason. They began experimenting with wood and vegetable ash glazes. She shared a subsequent partnership there with Norah Braden. After the war Beano moved to Kilmington Manor, Wiltshire where she continued potting until her death. She made functional stoneware thrown on a wheel, principally vases, bottles and bowls, with a sound sense of shape, and often relying solely on glaze for effect. She devoted herself to the study and recording of wood ash high fired stoneware glazes.

Her exhibitions included Paterson, Lefevre, and Little Galleries, Primavera, Craftsmen Potters Association, Kettles Yard.

Examples of her work can be seen at the Craft Study Centre, Bath, the Victoria and Albert Museum and Sudbury Hall.

Clive Bowen

Born in 1943 in Cardiff. Lives in Devon. Trained in painting and etching at Cardiff College of Art and trained as a potter under Michael Leach. For five years he worked at Brannams in Barnstaple making earthenware jugs and jars, then started his own pottery at Shebbear making domestic and kitchen ware and garden pots in local red earthenware. The pots may be decorated with three contrasting slips, using slip trailing, combing and sgraffito. They are fired once in a woodfired kiln to $1040°-1060°C$.

Major exhibitions include: Irving Gallery, Bideford; The Maker's Eye – Crafts Council; Craftsmen Potters Association; National Museum of Wales, Cardiff; Victoria and Albert Museum; Hambledon Gallery, Blandford Forum; Contemporary Applied Arts.

Norah Braden

Born in 1901. Studied art at the Central School and then at the Royal College. In 1925 went to St Ives as a potter becoming interested in wood ash glazing taught there by the Japanese Kiln technician Matsubayashi. Joined Katherine Pleydell Bouverie at her home, Coleshill, where they produced some outstanding stoneware pottery with various experimental wood ash glazes. She was described by Bernard Leach as perhaps his most naturally gifted pupil.

Norah Braden left Coleshill in 1936 to live on the South Coast. She taught at Brighton Art School carrying on after the war, though she had virtually given up potting in 1936. Her output was always small and she destroyed much of it.

Exhibited in major international exhibitions. Examples of her work in the Victoria and Albert Museum and the Crafts Study Centre Bath.

Alison Britton

Born in 1948 in Harrow. Lives in London. Trained at Leeds College of Art, Central School and the Royal College of Art where her contemporaries were Liz Fritsch, Jacqui Poncelet and Jill Crowley. She began her career decorating tiles. Tiles were followed by decorated jugs which she liked for the restriction of lip and handle. As her shapes became more three-dimensional, pictures gave way to abstract decoration painted with slips using brush and/or trailer, or slab built pots. She now makes vessels in earthenware in a less specific way, with stronger shapes, sometimes designed as pairs or groups. She is influenced by primitive textiles and the Japanese sense of asymmetric pattern in textiles.

Major exhibitions include: Amalgam, Barnes; Galerie het Kapelhuis, Amersfoort, Holland; Crafts Council, Victoria and Albert Museum; Sudbury Hall, Derbyshire; Prescote Gallery, London and Banbury; Westminster Gallery, Boston; Contemporary Applied Arts; Scottish Gallery, Edinburgh; Serpentine Gallery.

Work represented in many public collections in UK and overseas.

19

Hilary Brock

Born 1933 in Barry, South Wales. Lives in Leicestershire. Trained in illustration at Cardiff College of Art. After twelve years as a college senior lecturer in ceramics, he set up his own workshop in 1978, and became a full time potter.

His work is almost entirely figurative, based on a variety of historical periods, interpreted humorously and with a contemporary feeling. Earlier work was entirely stoneware. More recently work is modelled in stoneware and porcelain with on-glaze enamels. Hilary Brock is hoping to develop his work towards the use of earthenware clays on a larger scale.

Major exhibitions include: Peter Dingley, Stratford-upon-Avon; Norwich Museum; Open Eye Gallery, Edinburgh; Bluecoat Display Centre, Liverpool; Craftsmen Potters Association.

Christie Brown

Born in 1946 in Shipley, Yorkshire. Now living in London. After working as a domestic ware thrower and setting up a production pottery, Christie Brown trained at Harrow School of Art and moved away from domestic ware to hand-built figurative sculpture, influenced by classical, Egyptian and Renaissance sculptures.

All the work is in stoneware and the figures built from slabs, rolled and modelled, painted in vitreous slip and fired to 1140°C. Some are burnished and polished. Most are smoked. Christie Brown is exploring more complex methods of figure building, and plans to produce shortly a range of domestic earthenware.

Major exhibitions include: British Crafts Centre/Contemporary Applied Arts; Aspects Gallery, London; MCAD Gallery, Minneapolis; Oxford Gallery; Crafts Council; Amalgam, Barnes; Michaelson and Orient; Kingsgate Gallery, London.

21

Sandy Brown

Born in 1946 in Hampshire. Lives in Devon. At 22 she arrived in Japan where she discovered clay. She worked in the Daisei Pottery at Mashiko for three years, learning by watching. In 1973 she returned to England and set up her first studio. She has been artist in residence at the University of Texas, USA and Gippsland Institute, Australia. She is married to the Japanese potter Takeshi Yasuda. Sandy Brown's initial influence was Japanese Folk Pottery. Since then she has been influenced by abstract art and art as a means of expressing feelings and preserving sanity. She works in stoneware, with colourful glazes making handbuilt figures, thrown pieces, made with soft clay to emphasize its sensuality, and slab built pieces. She is progressing towards wall murals in tiles and clay pictures.

Major exhibitions include: Crafts Council, Victoria and Albert Museum; Beaux Arts, Bath; British Tableware, Dallas, Texas; Pat Barnes Gallery, USA; Wita Garinder Gallery, California; Oriel 31, Welshpool; Meat Market Craft Centre, Melbourne, Australia; Marianne Heller Gallery, West Germany.

Steve Buck

No mark used

Born in 1949 in Leeds. Now lives in London, and teaches ceramics part time in a comprehensive school. He attended the Harrow Studio Pottery Course 1979–1981 before setting up his studio. He is influenced by surrealism and Art Nouveau, by natural history and science fiction. His work is white earthenware, coiled or roughly shaped by building from pieces of clay. The textures are developed by painting with casting slip. They have an average of four or five firings. He colours with slips and underglaze pigment. His work explores the relationship of opposing forces.

Major exhibitions include: Anatol Orient, London; Museum of Worms, West Germany.

Work represented in public collections at the Victoria and Albert Museum and Cleveland County Museum.

Ian Byers

Born in 1947 in Birmingham. Now lives in Surrey. Studied at the Central School of Art under Dan Arbeid, Gordon Baldwin and Eileen Nisbit. Currently teaching part time at Hounslow and Bath Colleges. Influenced in his work by artists, particularly Picasso, and other potters, such as Paul Soldner, for the 'adventure' of their work.

He works principally in raku, but adopting whatever possibilities the work requires – part of the work may be in metal, or high fired for example. Pieces are hand-built, partly pressed, coiled and scraped, painted with fine slips then burnished, and fired to 1000°C.

Major exhibitions include: Galerie de Sluis, Holland; Anatol Orient; Galerie Charlotte Hennig, Darmstadt; Rufford Craft Centre; Bluecoat Display Centre, Liverpool; Craftsmen Potters Association.

Alan Caiger-Smith

Born in 1930 in Buenos Aires. Now lives in Berkshire. Trained at Camberwell School of Art and the Central School of Art and Design. He founded the Aldermaston Pottery in 1955 and has worked there continuously since with a small team of assistants and pupils.

The main influences on his work have been the European tin-glaze tradition, and Islamic pottery. He works in tin glazed earthenware with fired-in colours and smoked lustre. The forms are thrown, pressed and modelled, and mostly brush decorated. The majority is wood fired.

Major exhibitions include: Heals, London; Open Eye Gallery, Edinburgh; Oxford Gallery; Gardiner Museum, Toronto; City Museum, Stoke-on-Trent; Craftsmen Potters Association.

Work represented in public collections in UK and overseas.

Michael Cardew

1901–1983. After early experience of pottery with Edwin Beer Fishley, he worked with Bernard Leach for two years from 1923. He started making slipware and galena glazed earthenware at the Winchcombe Pottery which he acquired in 1926, then moving to Wenford Bridge Cornwall in 1939. In 1942 he took over from Harry Davis as pottery instructor at Achimota College, Gold Coast, and subsequently produced stoneware at Vumé-Dugamé, abandoning slip trailing for brush decoration. In 1948 at Wenford Bridge he turned over the production to stoneware. As pottery officer to the Nigerian Government (1950–65) he set up a pottery training centre at Abuja, Nigeria. He always made pots for use, with bold vigorous forms. A traditional craftsman, he fired with wood and explored the local environment for materials.

Major exhibitions include: Royal Institute Galleries 1931; Brygos Gallery, London, 1938; Berkeley Galleries, London; Paterson Gallery, London; Craftsmen Potters Association; Boymans Museum, Rotterdam; York City Art Gallery & Crafts Council; Aberystwyth Arts Centre.

Work represented in major public collections including Victoria and Albert Museum, University College of Wales and the Milner White Collection – York City Art Gallery.

26

Seth Cardew

Born in 1934 at Winchcombe. Now living at Wenford Bridge Pottery, Cornwall. Seth, son of Michael Cardew, studied painting at Chelsea School of Art and sculpture at Camberwell before working as a jobbing sculptor in the London film studios. He moved to Cornwall in 1970 to assist his father at Wenford Bridge which he took over in 1983 when Michael Cardew died. The pottery is now run as a family business.

All Seth Cardew's work is hand thrown or moulded stoneware, decorated by hand with brush, stick or comb, or slip trailer, then wood fired.

The pottery conducts courses for beginners, mid school and post graduate candidates, and has extensive library facilities for students of Michael Cardew.

Major exhibitions include: Fort Smith Art Center; Oxford Gallery; Heidelberg (Englische Keramik); Kingston Polytechnic; St Paul's School, Cirencester Workshop.

Peter Care

Born in 1952 in Kent. Now living in the Netherlands. Studied at Medway College of Art and Design and on leaving in 1973 taught ceramics and sculpture on the continent. He established a studio near Brussels in 1975. Returned to England between 1981 and 1988 and worked in the Cotswolds.

His pieces are hand-built, slab constructed from thin sheets or slabs of porcelain. Each section is a hollow form, the inner interlocking forms made while the slabs are still soft and pliable. Coloured slips and body stains are used. After firing to 1280°C the surface of each piece is polished and ground. The interlocking pieces can be arranged in various ways.

Major exhibitions include: Gallerie La Main, Brussels; Beaux Arts, Bath; Bohun Gallery, Henley on Thames; New Ashgate Gallery, Farnham; Peter Dingley, Stratford-upon-Avon; British Ceramic Art Transform, New york; Anatol Orient, London; Ingrid Presser, Geisenheim.

Daphne Carnegy

Born in 1947 in Lincolnshire. Now lives in London. After graduating and working as a teacher, and in publishing, she became apprenticed to a faience potter in France. In 1978 she began a course at Harrow School of Art and subsequently set up her own workshop in London. Now teaches part time at Harrow. Her work is tin-glazed earthenware, domestic ware and one-off larger pieces. They are thrown and turned and decorated by brush on the freshly applied glaze, using oxides and underglaze colours. Decoration is mainly brightly coloured fruit and floral designs.

Major exhibitions include: Amalgam, Barnes; New Ashgate Gallery, Farnham; Chestnut Gallery, Bourton-on-the-Water; Galerie Kunst und Handwerk, Berlin; Scottish Gallery; Bohun Gallery, Henley-on-Thames; Higher Street Gallery, Dartmouth; J K Hill, London; Contemporary Applied Arts, London.

Michael Casson

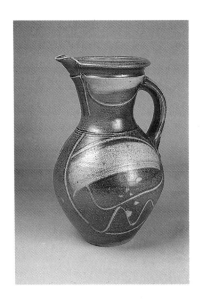

Born in 1925 in London. Now lives in Hereford and Worcester. Largely self-taught, but some training at Hornsey College of Art in the late 1940s. His earlier workshops were in central London and Buckinghamshire, before he and his wife Sheila Casson settled at Wobage Farm. Cofounder of the Studio Pottery Course at Harrow, and presenter of a BBC TV series, Craft of the Potter, in 1975. Now teaches History of Ceramics part time at Cardiff and holds workshops abroad, mainly in the USA.

He makes functional vessels, wheel thrown stoneware, mostly woodfired and salt glazed – jugs, bowls, jars, dishes and a range of teapots on legs.

Major exhibitions include: Craftsmen Potters Association; British Crafts Centre/Contemporary Applied Arts; Casson Gallery, London; St James' Gallery, Bath; Westminster Gallery, Boston; Ladygate Gallery, Beverley; Marianne Heller Gallery, Sandhausen.

Work represented in many public and private collections in the UK and abroad.

Sheila Casson

Born in 1930 in London. Now lives in Hereford and Worcester. Studied at Hornsey College of Art, and taught for two years before opening a workshop in London making tin glazed earthenware. In 1955 she married the potter Michael Casson, and in 1959 moved her workshop to Buckinghamshire, making mainly undecorated domestic ware.

They moved to their present workshop in 1977 where Sheila Casson makes more individual pieces of decorated porcelain and stoneware. Her influences are the surrounding landscape and the sense of pattern derived from early American Indian works and oriental carpets. Most work is thrown and turned on the wheel, decorated by inlay, paper resist and spray slips, and finally sgraffito before a gas firing. Some domestic ware made still, fired in a woodfired salt kiln.

Major exhibitions include: Newport Museum; 10 years at Wobage Farm; Candover Gallery, New Alresford; Craftsmen Potters Association; Stoke-on-Trent, Museum.

Bernard Charles

Born in 1930 in Shropshire. Now lives in West Sussex. Studied ceramics at Leicester and Stoke on Trent Colleges of Art in the late 1940s and early 1950s. Taught and lectured in ceramics and industrial design at Colleges and schools including Reading University, Poole School of Art and Benenden School. Now concentrates on making pots, distributed through galleries mainly in the South of England.

He works in porcellanous stoneware fired in an electric kiln. His thrown and turned forms with a textured surface are embellished with intaglio linear decoration. The decoration is important, carried out as the pot is made, and conceived as a whole.

Major exhibitions include: Beaux Arts, Bath; New Ashgate Gallery, Farnham; Terrace Gallery, Worthing; Candover Gallery, New Alresford; Primavera, Cambridge; Oxford Gallery; Sheila Harrison Fine Art.

Barbara Colls

Born in 1914 in Norwich. Studied at Norwich School of Art in the 1930s, and subsequently learnt pottery at Farnham School of Art in the 1950s and 1960s, part time, initially under Henry Hammond and Paul Barron, who encouraged the bird lidded pots. Returned to Norfolk in 1973 and maintains a small output of the same type of work.

She works in stoneware clays and porcelain. Pots are thrown and turned. The birds' heads, tails and wings are modelled. Coloured slips and coloured glazes are applied.

Major exhibitions include: Guildford House, Guildford, 1960s; Assembly House, Norwich; Norwich Castle Museum; Craftsmen Potters Association.

Christine Constant

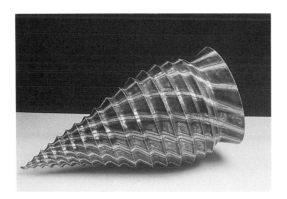

Born in 1958 in Bedford. Now lives in Tyne and Wear. Studied at Bedford College, Central School of Art and Design and Croydon College. She is resident craftsperson at Bensham Grove Community Centre, Gateshead, with part-time community classes related to this residency.

She works in various clays, semi-porcelain, raku, white and red earthenwares. Her pieces are made by a variety of methods: pressmoulding, casting, handbuilding, etc. They are partially glazed, raku fired and reduced in sawdust, with occasional use of glass and metallic lustre glazes. Her influences are a blend of the aquatic, geological and mechanical. As her work develops it is becoming less aggressive and architectural with gentler curves and livelier glazes.

Major exhibitions include: V & A Craft Shop; Keramic Studio, Vienna; Crafts Council Exhibition; Oxford Gallery; New Spirit in British Craft and Design, Los Angeles; Godfrey & Twatt, Harrogate; East-West Contemporary Ceramics, Seoul.

Joanna Constantinidis

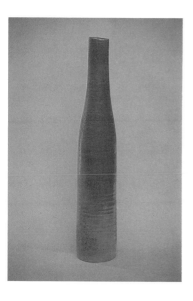

Born in 1927. Lives in Essex. Studied at Sheffield College of Art. She works in porcelain and stoneware. Her ceramic vessels are wheel thrown, usually as cylinders, without a base, then modified by modelling, pinching and cutting away. The surface is scraped and burnished with the back of a spoon, and sprayed with metal oxides then fired within saggars to produce lustrous surfaces. Her work is firmly allied to the vessel tradition. She is lecturer in Ceramics at Essex Institute of Higher Education, Chelmsford.

Major exhibitions include: Craftsmen Potters Association; Atmosphere, London; Beaux Arts, Bath; Oxford Gallery; Kettles Yard, Cambridge; New Art Forms, Chicago 1988; Crafts Council, Victoria and Albert Museum; Peter Dingley, Stratford-upon-Avon; Southampton Art Gallery.

Work represented in many public collections in UK and overseas.

Gordon Cooke

Born in 1949 in Manchester, where he still lives. Trained at Cheshire School of Art and Design and as a mature student after some years as a landscape designer. He now teaches part time at South Manchester Community College, and on residential courses at West Dean College, Chichester.

He works in porcelain and dark earthenware. His small scale pots are slab built using a method which exploits the tendency of clay to crack as it is rolled. On other occasions he uses textured clay fragments to build slabs which are finished with oxides and lustres.

Major exhibitions include: Casson Gallery, London; Cecilia Colman Gallery, London; Kettles Yard, Cambridge; Dan Klein, London; Galerie Luchien, Amsterdam; Westminster Gallery, Boston; Keramik Galerie Bowig, Hannover; Marianne Heller, Sandhausen.

Delan Cookson

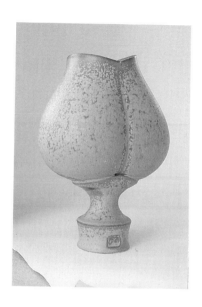

Born in 1937 in Torquay. Now lives in Buckinghamshire. Trained at Bournemouth College of Art and the Central School London and worked for a year under Ruth Duckworth. He taught ceramics full time between 1962 and 1988, when he decided to concentrate solely on his pottery. His interests have tended towards ceramic sculpture though he also makes individual and decorative pots.

He works in porcelain and stoneware, mostly throwing and turning. His sculptural work combines slab building, press moulding, coiling and throwing. Delan Cookson continues to develop ideas about individual forms, at present vessels.

Major exhibitions include: Galerie An Gross St Martin, Cologne; Bohun Gallery, Henley on Thames; St James' Gallery, Bath; Grape Lane Gallery, York; Whitworth Art Gallery; Rufford Crafts Centre; Brunel University; Victoria and Albert Museum.

Emmanuel Cooper

Born 1938 in Derbyshire. Lives in London, studied at Dudley Training College, Bournemouth School of Art and Hornsey School of Art. After working for Bryan Newman and Gwyn Hanssen he set up a pottery with two other potters in Notting Hill Gate in 1966. He moved to Finsbury Park in 1973, and to his present workshop in Primrose Hill in 1976. He teaches part time at Middlesex Polytechnic.

Emmanuel Cooper works in porcelain throwing and turning most of his pots, bowls and jugs. Some large flat dishes are press moulded. His pieces are fired at 1260°C in an electric kiln. He is developing some flatter open bowls, up to 24 inches in diameter.

He has been co-editor of the magazine *Ceramics Review* since 1969, and is the author of a number of books on pottery.

Major exhibitions include: Boadicea London 1968; British Crafts Centre/ Contemporary Applied Arts; Craftsmen Potters Shop; J K Hill, London; Victoria and Albert Museum.

Work represented in a number of public collections in the UK.

Hans Coper

1920-1981. Born in Germany, Hans Coper arrived in England shortly before the war. Hard labour took its toll on his health. In 1946 he joined Lucie Rie at Albion Mews making ceramic buttons, and very quickly developed the techniques of making pots. In the early years he and Lucie Rie made a wide range of elegant tableware in matt black and shiny white glazes. He began to explore sculptural forms and the influence of Picasso is evident in the decoration of some early pots. He was uninterested in colour; his pieces are predominantly dark brown, cream or matt black stoneware. By building up layers, and rubbing them down he achieved his complex surface textures, which he finished with burnishing. Moved to Somerset. Latterly due to illness he was restricted to making small pieces. These precise and poised forms are usually about 4 inches high, and among his best work. He taught at Camberwell and the Royal College of Art.

During his lifetime he exhibited regularly at the Berkeley Galleries London and at Primavera. In 1983 the Hans Coper Memorial Collection was installed at the Sainsbury Centre for Visual Arts, Norwich.

Gilles Le Corre

Born in 1956 in Quimper, France. Now lives in Oxford. Trained at Camberwell School of Arts and Crafts and worked for Janice Tchalenko before setting up his studio in Oxford. He teaches part time in a school and in adult education locally. His influences have evolved from an interest in functional ceramics and from the seascapes of his native Brittany. He works in stoneware, thrown on a wheel. Decoration is by means of brushes and slip trailing, adding layers of glazes to create a rich fusion of colours, fired to 1295°C.

Gilles Le Corre's work has developed towards more individual and decorative pieces and experimentation with new glazes.

Major exhibitions include: Contemporary Applied Arts; Oxford Gallery; Peter Dingley, Stratford-upon-Avon; The Scottish Gallery, Edinburgh; Rufford Crafts Centre; New Ashgate Gallery, Farnham; Craftsmen Potters Association.

Trevor Corser

Born in 1938 in Oldham. Lives at St Ives. Began work at the Leach Pottery, St Ives, in 1966 as a trainee assistant, with guidance from Bernard Leach and others. He later became senior potter in the team directed by Janet Leach, and is now the only remaining potter working with her.

Trevor Corser's pots clearly show the influence of Bernard and Janet Leach and Bill Marshall. His vases, bowls and bottles in porcelain and stoneware are thrown on a kick wheel and reduction fired in a gas kiln. He is at present working more with porcelain and experimenting with ash glazes.

Major exhibitions include: Amalgam, Barnes; Seibu Store, Tokyo; Beaux Arts, Bath; Rufford Craft Centre; Pro Art, St Louis, USA; Sirota Gallery; The English Gallery, West Germany; Penwith Society of Arts.

Philippa Cronin

PL

Born 1957 in Devon. Now lives in London. Studied Three Dimensional Design at Buckingham College of Higher Education, specializing in Silversmithing and metalwork. In 1981 she became ceramicist in residence at South Hill Park Arts Centre, Bracknell, and in 1984 set up her present studio. She has continued to teach both adults and children, for example in large scale community projects in London and in Holloway Prison.

She works predominantly in red earthenware, coiling and finishing by beating and scraping of the surfaces. Colour slips are applied in layers before and after biscuit firing. Final firing is to 1150°C. The figurative element in her work is becoming more apparent. She hopes to see this developing on a larger scale.

Major exhibitions include: Anatol Orient, London; Oxford Gallery; Kingsgate Gallery, London; New Ashgate Gallery, Farnham; Britain in Vienna Festival; Museum fur Kunst und Gewerbe, Hamburg; Craftsmen Potters Shop.

Jill Crowley

Signature

Born in Eire in 1946. Lives in London. Trained at Bristol Polytechnic and the Royal College of Art. She teaches part time at Morley College. Her ceramic satirical sculptures are handbuilt in raku, porcelain and oxidized stoneware. She builds up the clay by pinching and coiling. A heavily grogged clay gives a gravelly texture resistant to the shock of raku firing, and especially suitable for the portrait busts of pock-marked old men. Decoration contrasts smoked unglazed areas with those painted with slips and glaze, and the use of lustre.

Major exhibitions include: British Crafts Centre/Contemporary Applied Arts; Crafts Council, Victoria and Albert Museum; International Ceramics Competition, Faenza; Galerie L, Hamburg; Amalgam, Barnes; Darmstadt Museum; Somers Galerie, Heidelberg; Aspects, London; Michaelson and Orient, London; British Ceramics, Lazurus, Ohio.

Work represented in a number of public collections in UK and overseas.

43

Derek Davis

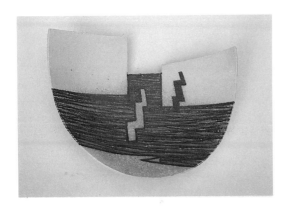

Born in 1926 in London. Lives in Arundel, West Sussex. Trained at the Central School of Arts and Crafts in 1945–1949 with Robert Buhler and Keith Vaughan as tutors. His influences are Picasso, Matisse and the American School of Painters.

He works in porcelain and stoneware, both thrown and hand moulded. His pieces are now mostly sculptural ceramics decorated in a figurative or symbolic manner as 'Observations on Life'.

Major exhibitions include: Sheila Harrison Fine Art; Blond Fine Art; Scottish Gallery, Edinburgh; Victoria and Albert Museum; Peter Dingley, Stratford-upon-Avon; Southampton Art Gallery; Keramion Museum, Frechen; Primavera, London and Cambridge; Craftsmen Potters Association.

Harry and May Davis

Harry Davis, born in 1910, died 1986, trained at Bournemouth Art School and met his wife May at the Leach Pottery in 1936. He was recruited from there by the Head of the Art School at Achimota College Ghana in 1937 to set up a pottery. By 1942 he had evolved a stoneware clay body from local clay and perfected a range of glazes from the local raw materials. Michael Cardew followed on, replacing Harry at the pottery. In 1949 Harry and Mary set up Crowan Pottery in Cornwall to make moderately priced stoneware for the table. In 1962 they emigrated to New Zealand and at Crewenna Pottery carried on the tradition though leaving for seven years in 1972 to start a pottery aid project in Peru. Harry Davis was a great improviser in the field of studio pottery, providing skills which have been of benefit particularly in developing countries.

Peter Dick

Born in 1936 in London. Now lives in York. He became interested in pottery while travelling around the world in the late 1950s. He was strongly influenced by Michael Cardew for whom he worked at Abuja, Northern Nigeria. On returning to England he worked for Ray Finch at Winchcombe for two years. In 1965 Peter Dick and his wife Jill set up the Coxwold Pottery in Yorkshire. They produce a wide range of work – mainly useful pots for house and garden, influenced by the country pottery of Europe. Their work is earthenware and low temperature stoneware, thrown, slip decorated and woodfired.

Frequent exhibitions at various venues including the Craftsmen Potters Association.

46

Mike Dodd

Born in 1943 in Surrey. Lives in Cumbria. Taught by Donald Potter at Bryanston School. After studying medicine at Cambridge and a post graduate year at Hammersmith College of Art he began his first pottery in Sussex. His present pottery was opened in 1986 when he ended a five year appointment as Head of the Pottery Department at Cumbria College of Art.

His work is reduction stoneware (occasionally porcelain) oil and wood fired. Almost all pots are thrown on the wheel. Local materials, clays, ochres, granites, etc, are used for slips and glazes. Mike Dodd is constantly seeking ways to improve glaze, decoration and form to increase the visual strength of the pots unobtrusively.

Major exhibitions include: Broughton Gallery, Lanarkshire; Amalgam, Barnes; Contemporary Applied Arts; Craftsmen Potters Association; Sussex and Brunel Universities; Osnabruck, Germany; North Cornwall Gallery and Museum.

Ruth Duckworth

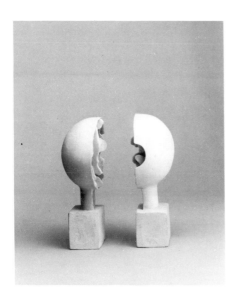

Born in 1919 in Hamburg. Arrived in England in 1936. Lives now in the United States. Her first contact with pottery was in 1953. A chance acquaintance with Lucie Ric led her to Hammersmith School of Art and the Central School where Hans Coper was a strong influence on her. Her early pottery in the late 1950s was tableware, light shapes thrown on the wheel, in her studio near Kew Gardens. Then she began to turn towards delicate pinched porcelain, heavy coiled ovoid pots in stoneware with rough partially glazed surfaces, and semi-figurative sculptures. In 1964 she went as visiting professor of Ceramics to Chicago, where she remains. She has made a number of large scale mural pieces to commission which reflect the influence of earth sciences. She still makes small scale porcelain pieces reminiscent of stones and bones which are rolled, scraped, and sanded and sometimes held together by porcelain pins.

She has exhibited regularly in America and outside. Her most recent major show in England took place in 1987 at Contemporary Applied Arts, London.

Work represented in public collections in UK, Germany, Holland, Italy, Japan and USA.

John Dunn

Born in 1944 in London. Lives in Sussex. He works in raku, making large dishes 23 inches in diameter, as he has done for the last few years. He is single minded about the development of this form which he is still refining. His dishes are coiled, and his glazes are of vibrant colours, prompted by some of the qualities of hand made glass. His new work, an extension of the large dish, is square with bright coloured hi-tech graphic mirages. A new ultra light weight raku kiln enables John Dunn easily to undertake raku demonstrations abroad.

Major exhibitions include: Rufford Craft Centre, Nottinghamshire; Craftsmen Potters Association; Museum of Ceramics, Barcelona; EP Galeries, Dusseldorf; Galerie Le Sorbier, Paris; Chelsea Crafts Fair.

Ruth Dupré

Born in 1954 in Essex. Now living in London. Trained at Ravensbourne College and Hornsey College of Art. Since leaving college she has travelled widely in South America, Kenya and India and her work has been influenced by the textiles and costumes of the contries she has visited. She is a regular visiting lecturer at Croydon College of Art. The basic forms of her pieces are slabbed, though a variety of methods is used in each. Surfaces are very textured, and colours applied at every stage. Recent pieces have combined function and decoration – for example, dishes shaped as birds.

Major exhibitions include: Open Eye Gallery, Edinburgh; Anatol Orient, London; New Ashgate Gallery, Farnham; Westminster Gallery, Boston; MCAD Gallery, Minneapolis; Crafts Council, Victorial and Albert Museum; Aspects Gallery, London; Contemporary Applied Arts; Manchester City Art Gallery.

Geoffrey Eastop

Born in 1921 in London. Now living in Berkshire. Studied painting at Goldsmiths College and Academie Ranson, Paris. After six years at the Aldermaston Pottery with Alan Caiger Smith set up his own studio in Berkshire, and for a time collaborated with John Piper.

Until 1985 his work was principally thrown and modelled stoneware and porcelain with an emphasis on form. Since then he has begun to research the use of vitreous slips to develop the possibilities of a painterly approach to ceramics. His work is becoming larger and relying more than formerly on the spontaneity of brushwork. Influences are often ethnic and primitive, but include modern art, and the forms and markings on animals and plants.

Major exhibitions include: National Museum of Wales; British Crafts Centre; Bohun Gallery, Henley-on-Thames; Beaux Arts, Bath; Bluecoat Display Centre, Liverpool; Potters Gallery, Stuttgart.

Work represented in a number of public collections in the UK.

51

David Eeles

Born in 1933 in London. Now lives in Dorset. Studied at Willesden School of Art under Helen Pincombe. He ran a workshop in North London for six years before moving to his present studio in Dorset, which operated as a family workshop. David Eeles works in earthenware, stoneware and porcelain, firing in oil and wood, but he is moving more towards wood-fired stoneware and porcelain. Decoration may be painted, glaze trailed, wax resist, papercut, etc.

Recent major exhibitions include: Arts Study Centre, Wycombe Abbey School; Craftsmen Potters Association.

Work represented in a number of public collections in UK and overseas.

Siddig El' Nigoumi

Born 1931 in Sudan. Now lives in Farnham, Surrey. Studied Arts and Crafts at Khartoum Art School in the early 1950s and was selected for further training at the Central School of Arts and Crafts in London. Though he returned to work at the Khartoum Art School, essential improvements were slow to materialize and Siddig El' Nigoumi settled in Britain, joining the staff of the West Surrey College of Art and Design where he still works.

His work is stoneware and earthenware often decorated with scratched and sgraffito designs and burnished to a fine shiny surface. Pots are thrown and plates are made in plaster moulds. His forms and decoration have a distinctly African flavour but modern technology and recent events are often his subject matter.

Major exhibitions include: New Grafton Gallery, London; Craftsmen Potters Association; Aberystwyth Arts Centre; Victoria and Albert Museum; New Ashgate Gallery, Farnham; Peter Potter Gallery, Dunbar; British Crafts Centre/Contemporary Applied Arts; Oriel 31, Welshpool.

Derek Emms

Born in 1929 in Lancashire. Now lives in Staffordshire. Trained at Accrington School of Arts and Crafts and Leeds College of Art. After national service he worked for a year at the Leach Pottery under Bernard and David Leach. Between 1955 and 1985 he was a full time lecturer in ceramics at the North Staffordshire Polytechnic. He retired in 1985 to devote more time to his own work.

He works in stoneware and porcelain, throwing and turning functional ware and individual pieces. All are fired to 1280°C in a gas kiln. He decorates by engraving or with brush decoration. The elements of nature in the countryside are used as a source of ideas for patterns.

Major exhibitions include: Craftsmen Potters Association; Arts and Crafts Exhibition Society; Red Rose Guild; Rufford Craft Centre.

Dorothy Feibleman

Born in 1951 in Indiana, USA. Lives in London. Studied at Rochester Institute of Technology. She has been living and working in Britain since the early 1970s. She first started laminating clay after a trip to Los Angeles in order to make laminated beads. Her work is small in scale and incorporates extremly fine decoration. Rods and slices of laminated clays are built up and finely sliced to construct the pot formed inside a bowl which is used as a mould. After drying, the bowl is removed and the outer layer scraped away before firing.

Major exhibitions include: Primavera; Galerie L, Hamburg; Contemporary Applied Arts; Craftsmen Potters Association; Casson Gallery, London; New Ashgate Gallery, Farnham; Oxford Gallery; Charlotte Hennig, Darmstadt; Henry Rothschild Collection; Indiana University Art Museum.

Work represented in many public collections in USA and Europe.

Ray Finch

Born in 1914 in London. Lives at Winchcombe, Gloucestershire. Trained with Dora Billington at the Central School of Arts and Crafts in 1935 and with Michael Cardew at Winchcombe from 1936 to 1939. He purchased and restarted the Winchcombe pottery after the war in 1946 and has worked there ever since with a team of four or five assistants.

From 1946 until 1960 the pottery made slipware, since 1960 stoneware. A wide range of useful domestic pottery is handthrown and fired in a large wood fired kiln. The emphasis both in standard ware, and individual pieces, is for making pots which are both to be used and enjoyed.

Major exhibitions include: Craftsmen Potters Association including opening exhibitions in 1960; International Ceramics, Faenza; Craft Council; British Council Exhibitions to Iran, Egypt and Hong Kong; Stoke City Art Gallery and Museum; Michael Cardew and Pupils, York; Chestnut Gallery, Bourton-on-the-Water.

Jutka Fischer

Born in 1949 in Hungary. Lives in East Sussex. After studying pottery in California she came to England in 1970 and took pottery classes at the Camden Art Centre under Mohammed Abdalla, followed by three years at the Central School of Art and Design. Jutka Fishcher ran a gallery in Sussex exhibiting the work of various artists and craftsmen. She now teaches part time at a comprehensive school.

Her inspiration comes from early industrial pottery and fabrics and textiles. She works in white earthenware and body colours making pots by overlapping pieces of coloured clay, and forming shapes by moulding or slabbing. Decoration is mostly inlaid. She is currently working on larger pieces and murals for gardens.

Major exhibitions include: Contemporary Applied Arts; New Ashgate Gallery, Farnham; Harvey Nichols, Knightsbridge; Woodstock County Museum; Norwich Art Centre; Amalgam, Barnes; Craftsmen Potters Association; Camden Arts Centre, London.

57

Bernard Forrester

Born in 1908 in Stoke-on-Trent. Lives in Devon. Apprenticed at Mintons, Stoke-on-Trent as a modeller. After studying painting and drawing at Newcastle upon Tyne he became Art and Craft Teacher at Dartington Hall School, Devon. In 1952 he set up his own pottery in South Devon and continues to work there full time.

His work is porcelain and stoneware, thrown and turned with incised line drawing decoration, woodash glazed and painted in lustres and burnished gold.

Major exhibitions include: Piccadilly Gallery, 1955; Kettles Yard, Cambridge; Gallery 359, Nottingham; Westminster Gallery, Boston; Ladygate Gallery, Beverley; St James' Gallery, Bath; Gallery 88, Totnes; Dartington Hall, Totnes.

Work represented in a number of public collections in the UK.

Robert and Sheila Fournier

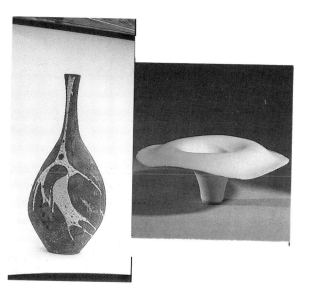

Robert Fournier was born in 1915 in London. Trained at the Central School of Arts and Crafts, and worked as assistant to Dora Billington from 1946 to 1950, while building a house and pottery in Hertfordshire. Started the Pottery Department at Goldsmiths College in 1950. Sheila, born 1930, was a student there. After running Castle Hill Pottery in Kent between 1964 and 1971 they set up the Fournier Pottery at Lacock, Wiltshire, from which they retired in 1986.

They worked in all materials from sawdust firmings to rough raku earthenware, stoneware and porcelain. 'Useful' ware was thrown, one-off pieces generally handbuilt. They built all their own equipment from wheels to kilns, and wrote a number of books on pottery.

Major exhibitions include: Sussex University; St Albans; Primavera, Cambridge; St James Gallery, Bath; Craftsmen Potters Association.

Valerie Fox (formerly Val Barry)

va B

Born in 1937 in South Yorkshire. Now lives in London. Studied ceramics at Sir John Cass School of Art, London. She set up a studio in London in 1970 and for fourteen years made sculptural pieces in stoneware and porcelain, slab building in subtle muted colours. Her pots were finely balanced and similar to blades, sails, slender bones and seed pods.

In 1984 she studied bronze technique, and now works solely to commission in bronze.

Major exhibitions include: Peter Dingley, Stratford-upon-Avon Barclaycraft, Brighton; Oxford Gallery; Bohun Gallery, Henley-on-Thames; Graham Gallery, New York; Pennsylvania State University Museum; International Ceramics, Italy.

Work represented in many public collections.

Ruth Franklin

Born in 1948 in London. Trained at Hornsey and Croydon Colleges of Art, and Harrow College of Higher Education. Her early work in porcelain incorporated, through her love of drawing, animals, washing lines, TVs, the London underground, tourists, etc. Her work was thrown, turned, then cut out to form symbols and objects related to the decoration. In 1981 she made a series of slab-built masks, held together with nuts and bolts – a combination of painting and pottery. Gradually she introduced pieces of wood and metal. In 1983 she stopped working in clay and began with wood. Picasso is a strong influence in her work.

Major exhibitions include: Craftsmen Potters Association; Casson Gallery, London; Oxford Gallery; Katherine House Gallery, Marlborough; Aspects, London; Sunderland Arts Centre.

David Frith

Born in 1943 in Ashton-under-Lyne. Lives in Denbigh, North Wales
Trained at Wimbledon School of Art and Stoke-on-Trent School of Ar
under Derek Emms. In 1963 he set up his first workshop in Denbigh
producing feather combed slipware dishes. The workshop developed
assistants were taken on, and in 1975 David Frith moved to his presen
pottery, an old woollen mill, where he and his wife Margaret make ?
range of standard ware, as well as their own individual pots. Davic
Frith's pieces are predominantly thrown in stoneware and porcelain
some beaten and faceted to give surfaces for decoration. Decoration i?
with wax or wax and painted pigments, or sometimes simply ?
combination of glazes gives the surface quality.

Major exhibitions include: Craftsmen Potters Assocition; Bluecoa'
Display Centre, Liverpool; Bohun Gallery, Henley-on-Thames; Newpor
Museum and Art Gallery; Aberystwyth Arts Centre; Keramik Galerie
Bowig, Hannover; Rufford Craft Centre; Ladygate Gallery, Beverley
Chestnut Gallery, Bourton-on-the-Water.

Elizabeth Fritsch

No mark used.
All work recorded photographically.

Born in 1940 in Shropshire. Lives in London. Studied music at Birmingham School of Music and Royal Academy, and Pottery at the Royal College of Art under Hans Coper. For a year she worked in Denmark, holding her first solo exhibition in Copenhagen. Her forms are vessels but never utilitarian. They are hand built in stoneware with decoration integral to the pot, using precise geometrical patterns to contrive optical games. Their surfaces have a natural matt texture. They are painted with slip often in earth colours, and given numerous colour firings. Colour is becoming increasingly important in her work. She is influenced by music, especially ethnic and jazz, by early Italian frescos and the art of ancient civilizations, and by mathematics and geology.

Major exhibitions include: Crafts Council; British Crafts Centre/ Contemporary Applied Arts; International Ceramics Competition – Poland; Travelling Exhibitions 'Pots about Music' – Leeds City Art Galleries; British Art and Design, Vienna; Fischer Fine Art, London; British Artist Craftsmen in Kyoto – British Council.

Work represented in many public collections in UK and overseas.

Annette Fuchs

Born in 1939 in Knutsford, Cheshire. Now living in Oxfordshire. Trained at the Royal Salford Technical College School of Art, and Camberwell School of Art. To gain practical experience worked at the Briglin Pottery before joining her sister in a joint studio in London. In 1965 she set up her own present pottery near Henley-on-Thames.

She works in earthenware, stoneware and porcelain, throwing individual pieces and domestic ware with a wide range of subtle glazes. Her pots are fired between 1060° and 1285°C. Her current work is developing towards simpler lines and forms.

Major exhibitions include: Craftsmen Potters Shop; Seibu Stokes, Tokyo; Boadicea, London; Pennsylvania State University Museum; Barclaycraft, Brighton; Terrace Gallery, Worthing; Courtyard Gallery, Cheltenham.

Tessa Fuchs

Born in 1936 in Cheshire. Now lives in Surrey. Studied at Salford Art School and Central School of Arts and Crafts, London. Then set up a studio to make sculptural pieces and some domestic ware, inspired by her interest in animals, plants, trees and landscape. She teaches part time at Putney School of Art. She works in red earthenware fired to 1080°C. Her sculptural forms are assembled using slabbed and coiled parts. Colourful matt glazes are applied to achieve a varied finish. Work is becoming larger and more sculptural.

Major exhibitions include: Oxford Gallery; New Ashgate Gallery, Farnham; Bohun Gallery, Henley-on-Thames; Ladygate Gallery, Beverley; Galerie Charlotte Hennig, Darmstadt; Kettles Yard, Cambridge; British Crafts Centre/Contemporary Applied Arts; Craftsmen Potters Association.

Work represented in a number of museums and public collections.

Geoffrey Fuller

No mark used

Born in 1936 in Derbyshire. Lives there now. Worked as a librarian in Sheffield until 1965 when, following a year's foundation course he trained on the BA Ceramics Course at Farnham School of Art. Between 1972 and 1987, while rebuilding his house and workshop, he taught in a number of posts but principally on the vocational Ceramics Course at Chesterfield College of Art. Resigned in 1987 to work full time as a potter.

Geoffrey Fuller works in earthenware clay, fired between 1040 and 1100°C, making both useful pots such as bowls and jugs, which are generally thrown, and slabbed figures. His clay is used as directly as possible and decorated with coloured slips and a clear glaze.

Major exhibitions include: Primavera, London 1969; British CraftsCentre/ Contemporary Applied Arts; Amalgam, Barnes; Stafford City Art Gallery; Darmstadt Design Institute, Germany; Craftsmen Potters Association; Copernican Connection, Beverley.

David Garland

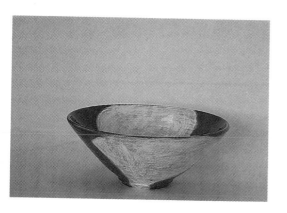

Born in 1941 in Northamptonshire and spent his childhood in New Zealand. Now lives in Cheltenham. He is a painter who makes pots. He has had no formal training in ceramics and only began potting at the age of 30. He makes cups, bowls, plates, jugs and teapots, thrown in red or buff earthenware and coated in a creamy slip, and decorated with oxide. Lines are scratched through to reveal the clay beneath. Decoration may be abstract, but sometimes calligraphic figures are used. David Garland's influences are early English Pottery, the work of other potters, guitar music and jazz.

Major exhibitions include: Oxford Gallery; Oriel Gallery, Welshpool; Amalgam, Barnes; Crafts Council; Contemporary Applied Arts; Chicago Art Fair; Peterborough Museum and Art Gallery; Contemporary British Crafts Kyoto and Tokyo.

Work represented in a number of collections in UK.

Marian Gaunce

Born in 1945 in Devon and now living in Surrey. She trained as a potter at Croydon College of Art and set up her own studio in 1980.

She works in porcelain, making mainly bowls. Slabs are formed with coloured clay, then press moulded in one, two or three piece moulds. After initial firing the pieces are sanded down, and refired to 1220–1240°C.

Major exhibitions include: Bohun Gallery, Henley-on-Thames; Graham Gallery, New York; British Crafts Centre/Contemporary Applied Arts; Martha Schneider Gallery, Chicago; Queensberry Hunt Studios, London; Rosenthal Studio, Hamburg.

Work represented in public collections in UK and America.

Ian Godfrey

No mark used

Born in 1941 in London. Lives there now. Studied at Camberwell School of Art and Crafts under Ian Auld, Hans Coper and Lucie Rie. In 1962 he set up his first workshop in London. There followed part time teaching at Camberwell and a research fellowship at the Royal College of Art. His sources have been oriental and mediterranean with a mixture of symbols combined and arranged together. His forms in a mixture of clays are made on the wheel then cut and scored with a penknife into temples, animals, birds, flowers, etc. He uses the same tool to cut his perforated bowls after throwing and turning. Glazes have very little colour. He is working privately on a new range of work.

Major exhibitions include: Primavera, London 1960s; Quantas Gallery, London; British Crafts Centre, London; International Exhibition of Ceramics, Faenza; Heals, London; Keramion in Frechen, Germany; Overseas exhibitions in Stuttgart, Stockholm, Osaka, Antwerp, Japan.

Work represented in a number of public collections in UK and overseas.

Ian Gregory

Born in 1942 in London. Now lives in Dorset. Self taught, Ian Gregory started a workshop in 1974 making earthenware flower containers, tiles and domestic ware. He started salt glazing and developing woodfired kilns, and his book, *Kiln Building* (Pitman, 1977), led to teaching opportunities at Bath Academy of Art, Cardiff and Medway Schools of Art. He now teaches art and ceramics at Milton Abbey School, Dorset. His early influences were the Martin brothers and Fulham Pottery. They are now early Greek and Roman Art. Ian Gregory works in porcelain and salt glazed stoneware. Most work is slip glazed, and some enamelled in a later firing. His work is developing towards figurative sculpture.

Major exhibitions include: Craftsmen Potters Association; British Crafts Centre/Contemporary Applied Arts; Beaux Arts, Bath; The Gallery, Dorchester; Casson Gallery, London; Primavera, Cambridge; Oxford Gallery; Victoria and Albert Museum; Bluecoat Centre, Liverpool.

70

Arthur Griffiths

Born in 1928 in Wolverhampton. Lives in Leicestershire. Studied at Wolverhampton College of Art and worked subsequently at Crowan Pottery for Harry Davis, and at the Leach Pottery St Ives. In 1954 he took over the Ceramics Department at Loughborough College of Art from David Leach and remained in charge there until 1983 when he took early retirement and returned to his own work.

He makes a small range of domestic ware and individual pieces with an emphasis on form rather than decoration. He works in stoneware and porcelain, throwing and turning, and with some hand building of large pieces.

Major exhibitions include: Bradford City Art Gallery; Penwith Gallery, St Ives; Midland Group Gallery, Nottingham; 359 Gallery, Nottingham; Marie Jordan Gallery, Wakefield; Nottingham Castle Museum.

Linda Gunn-Russell

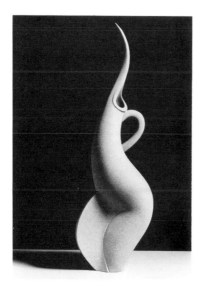

Born in 1953 in London. Living in London. Trained at Camberwell School of Arts and Crafts. Her forms are artificially flattened vessels with domestic associations, but never functional. The teapot is a favourite with spout and handle offering endless possibilities for distortion. The pots are made in sections from leather-hard pieces cut out of sheets of clay. The decoration is applied at various stages before and after firing. She generally decorates with slip applied by brush because it lends itself to precision and control. Her ideas may originate with magazine cut-outs, clothes, paintings, plants or fossils.

Major exhibitions include: Bohun Gallery, Henley-on-Thames; Amalgam, Barnes; British Crafts Centre/Contemporary Applied Arts; Anatol Orient, London; Garth Clark, New York; Bourne Fine Art, Edinburgh; Nieman Marcus Dallas and San Francisco; Westminster Gallery, Boston; Dorothy Weiss, Los Angeles.

Work represented in a number of public collections in UK and USA.

Thomas Samuel Haile

1908–1948. Went to the Royal College of Art as a painter in 1931. Came under the influence of Staite Murray and pottery became an extension of his painting. Although pots from his Brygos exhibition in 1937 were bought by Milner White, the Contemporary Art Society and museums, he only enjoyed real success in the USA where he taught during the war, and where his surrealist style appealed. He was appointed pottery instructor at the University of Michigan in 1942, but subsequently drafted into the US Army and transferred to the British Army in 1944. On demobilization in 1945 he made slip decorated earthenware at Sudbury in Suffolk, and moved in 1947 to Shinner's Bridge, Dartington. The next year he was killed in a motorcycle accident. The potter Marianne de Trey is his widow. His stoneware pots, often with titles, were decorated with figurative brushwork in the style of contemporary painting and sculpture. His work is represented in collections in Europe and the USA. Examples of his work can be seen in the Milner White Collection at York City Art Gallery and Southampton Art Gallery.

Jane Hamlyn

Born in 1940 in London. Lives in Yorkshire. Trained at Harrow School of Art with Michael Casson. She set up her present workshop in 1975, producing salt glazed stoneware functional pots, both for use and for ornament. She is influenced by the European ceramic tradition and is keen to develop the potential of the salt glaze process. Jane Hamlyn's pots are decorated with coloured slips and modelled handles. She is developing her work towards more colour, impressed textures and combined thrown and slabbed techniques.

Major exhibitions include: Saltsbrand 86, Koblenz; Aberystwyth Arts Centre; Contemporary Applied Arts, London; Leeds City Art Gallery; European Arts & Crafts, Stuttgart; Saltglaze, Budapest; New Ashgate Gallery, Farnham; St James' Gallery, Bath.

Henry Hammond

1914-1989. He studied at the Royal College of Art under Staite Murray, and after war service with Bernard Leach and Michael Cardew. He lived in Farnham where he was for a number of years Head of Three Dimensional Design at West Surrey College of Art and Design. He shared a studio nearby with Paul Barron until Paul's death.

Henry Hammond's work includes both stoneware and porcelain thrown and turned with brush decoration, in combinations of iron, cobalt, and chrome oxides. The pots are twice fired. They are principally bowls and vases and many are decorated with fish, grasses, reeds, dragonflies and birds.

Major exhibitions include: Brygos Gallery, London; Primavera, London; Kettles Yard, Cambridge; The Thirties Exhibition, Hayward Gallery, London; Craftsmen Potters Association; New Ashgate Gallery, Farnham; The Casson Gallery, London; Contemporary British Pottery, Hong Kong.

Work represented in a number of public collections in UK and overseas.

Peter Hayes

Born in 1946 in Birmingham, lives in Bath. Trained as a potter at Birmingham College of Art and spent some years in Africa working for the British Council establishing and developing pottery and craft centres. In 1982, returned to England and set up a studio in a converted toll bridge by the Avon. In 1984 headed a mission to Japan and South Korea with a group of Indian potters to investigate new techniques. He works in many different clays fired to temperatures between 1100 and 1280°C. By building up textured clays and burnishing and polishing he contrasts rough and smooth finishes to give effects ranging from weathered clay to leather.

Major exhibitions include: Peter Dingley, Stratford-upon-Avon; New Ashgate Gallery, Farnham; Scottish Gallery, Edinburgh; Leigh Gallery, London; Courcoux and Courcoux, Salisbury; Graham Gallery, New York; New Art Forms, Chicago; Sheila Harrison Fine Art; Salt House Gallery, St Ives; Oxford Gallery.

Ewen Henderson

Born in 1934 in Staffordshire. Lives in London. In 1964 he resigned as manager of a timber preservation company in South Wales, and took up painting. He was trained at Goldsmiths College where he was drawn to clay, and at Camberwell under Hans Coper and Lucie Rie. He now teaches at Camberwell and Goldsmiths.

His inspirations have been Korea and the East, and now North American Indians. He thinks of himself as a sculptor rather than a potter. His pieces are handbuilt forms made up of different clays and laminated. The different clays shrink at different rates when fired, warping, cracking and fusing. Decorated in muted organic colours, they may be fired many times.

Major exhibitions include: Peter Dingley, Stratford-upon-Avon; Graham Gallery, New York; Oxford Gallery; Contemporary Applied Arts, London; Westminster Gallery, Boston; Atmosphere, Zurich; Garth Clark, Chicago, San Francisco; Kyoto and Tokyo, British Council; Galerie Besson, London.

Work represented in numerous public collections in UK and overseas.

Karin Hessenberg

Born in 1944 in Berkhamsted. Lives in London. Karin Hessenberg worked in medical research before training at Camberwell School of Arts and Crafts where Lucie Rie was a tutor. She is a part time secondary school art teacher, an occasional teacher at Medway College of Design and holds sculpture and pottery evening classes. Most of her work is porcelain, thrown and turned. Rims and handles are handbuilt. Some pieces are decorated with an orange London Clay slip, and are burnished and sawdust fired to give a tortoiseshell effect. Some are glazed and fired to 1250°C in an electric kiln. She is developing an interest in larger works for outdoors, with different clays and slips.

Major exhibitions include: Henry Rothschild, Biennial; British Crafts Centre/Contemporary Applied Arts; Kettles Yard, Cambridge; Oxford Gallery; Westminster Gallery, Boston; Keramik Studio, Vienna; Crafts Council; Craft & Design Centre, Leeds City Art Gallery.

Nicholas Homoky

Born in 1950 in Hungary. Lives in Bristol. He came to England at the age of six. Trained at Bristol Polytechnic and the Royal College of Art. He is primarily concerned with the vessel, its volume and space. Until recently his work has been in white polished porcelain, thrown and turned and finished with black painted rims and designs inlaid with stained black porcelain slip. His recent work is in red clay, burnished and raw fired. The bottles or vases are slab built or thrown. In some cases the pots are decorated with the same shapes as the pots themselves. Spouts, handles, lids and rims are applied in relief or as inlay.

Major exhibitions include: Convergence Gallery, New York; Henry Rothschild – Primavera exhibition in Germany; Oxford Gallery; Westminster Gallery, Boston; Crafts Council, Victoria and Albert Museum; Beaux Arts, Bath; Newport Museum and Art Gallery; Scottish Gallery; Queensberry Hunt Studio, London; Keramik Galerie Bowig, Hannover.

Work represented in many public collections in the UK and overseas.

Anita Hoy

Studied at Copenhagen School of Art 1933–37. Returning to England in 1939 she joined Bullers Limited at Stoke-on-Trent starting a studio department within the factory making porcelain with high temperature glazes. The studio grew from a one person workshop to ten in 1950. The prototype was designed and executed by Anita Hoy then passed to the team. The ware was exhibited at the Festival of Britain exhibition but the department was not run on commercial lines and closed in 1952. She then joined Royal Doulton at Lambeth as a designer of saltglazed stoneware. Since 1957 she has produced individual pieces in porcelain and subsequently stoneware in her own studio. Her decoration comprises carving, coloured slips and oxide brushwork under or over clear glazes.

Major exhibitions include: Craftsmen Potters Association; Bullers Exhibition at Gladstone Pottery Museum; Doulton Story, Victoria and Albert Museum.

Work represented in a number of public collections in the UK.

Neil Ions

Born 1949 in Newcastle-under-Lyme. Lives in Gloucestershire. Trained in Sculpture at Newport College of Art 1969–72 and the Royal College of Art. A founder member of a group workshop set up in 1975 at Stow-on-the-Wold. Present workshop set up in 1982.

Major influences in his work are studies of wildlife and American Indian artefacts. He works in earthenware clay painted with slips, by coiling, press moulding, slabbing and extruding. His work is developing with larger, more sculptural pieces, still figurative and usually including a musical component.

Major exhibitions include: Crafts Council; Leigh Gallery, London; Blue Coat Centre, Liverpool; St James Gallery, Bath; Craftsmen Potters Association; Cirencester Workshops.

John Jelfs

Born in 1946 in Devon. Lives in Gloucestershire. He trained as a marine engineer and went to sea for two years. Then he discovered pottery. He is largely self taught, his only formal training being a foundation course at Cheltenham. His present workshop was established in 1973 in Bourton-on-the-Water where until 1976 he made earthenware. He works with his wife who is a sculptor and potter, making stoneware and porcelain domestic ware and one off pieces. His domestic ware is made in the traditional way, throwing and turning and decorating with slips and glazes. His one off pieces are thrown, cut and reassembled, slipped and combed. His work is becoming more sculptural and less functional.

Major exhibitions include: Bluecoat Display Centre, Liverpool; Chestnut Gallery, Bourton-on-the-Water; Craftsmen Potters Association; Oriel 31, Welshpool; Tokyo Store, Tokyo; Victoria and Albert Museum, CPA Anniversary.

82

David Lloyd Jones

Born in 1928 in Wimbledon. Now lives in York. His first encounter with pottery was in India in the late 1940s when he was in the Army and saw pots being made by hand in village workshops. Not until the age of 34 did he begin to make pots himself. He makes a full range of tableware and a variety of individual items – sometimes large plates or pots, always vessels.

David Lloyd Jones works in stoneware and porcelain. The majority of his pieces are thrown, but some are slab built and he is developing ideas for slab construction with texture, principally for salt glazing. He uses a large oilfired kiln, and a small wood fired one for occasional salt glazing.

Has exhibited widely in the UK and to a lesser extent abroad. His work is in public collections including:

Victoria and Albert Museum; Fitzwilliam Museum, Cambridge; Crafts Council Collection; Glasgow Museum; Stoke-on-Trent Museum; Belgian State Collection, Brussels; Kunstindustrimuseum, Bergen, Norway.

Mo Jupp

M|O
U|B

Born in 1938 in London where he lives now. Trained at Camberwell under Hans Coper, Lucie Rie, Ian Auld and Bryan Newman and at the Royal College of Art. He has worked from various studios in the Gloucestershire area including a 15th century farmhouse and a manorhouse, and he still teaches every week at Bristol Polytechnic, Bath Academy of Art, Middlesex Polytechnic and Harrow Pottery Course.

He makes sculptured ceramics and works with any materials that can be fired, using a variety of methods. Firstly producing helmets in stoneware, then busts of women. His latest works, still on the theme of women, are slender figures and torsoes.

Major exhibitions include: Primavera, London and Cambridge; 1s Triennale of Ceramics, Belgrade; Arts Council Shows in Japan and USA Oxford Gallery; British Crafts Centre/Contemporary Applied Arts Victoria and Albert Museum, London; Westminster Gallery, Boston Aberystwyth Arts Centre.

Jill Fanshawe Kato

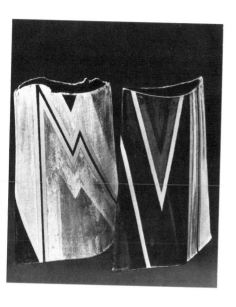

Born in Nottingham. Now lives in North London. Jill Fanshawe Kato graduated from Chelsea Art School in painting. She lived for six years in Japan and studied pottery intensively at the School of Bizen potter Yosei Itaka and at Musoan Koratsu Pottery School in Tokyo. She produces functional pots for Japanese and English use and creates sculptural ceramics. She teaches pottery at Goldsmiths' College.

Jill Fanshawe Kato works in stoneware, mainly slab built, but also coiled and thrown. She uses slips, underglazes and glazes much as a painter uses paint, in a variety of decorative methods. Her ceramic sculptures are becoming larger and more abstract. They are inspired by mountains.

Major exhibitions include: Ad Hoc Gallery, Tokyo; Keio Department Store, Tokyo; Primavera, Cambridge; New Ashgate Gallery, Farnham; Leigh Gallery, London; Gaku, Tokyo; Oxford Gallery; Norwich Castle Museum.

Walter Keeler

Born in 1942 in London. Lives at Penallt, Monmouth. Studied at Harrow School of Art under Victor Margrie, and established his first studio in Buckinghamshire making oxidized stoneware and oil fired saltglaze. After a period making raku he turned to the development of salt glaze techniques, experimenting with various kilns and firing processes. He teaches part time at Bristol Polytechnic. His work is functional stoneware thrown on the wheel, and then adapted. Form is paramount. His fascination for metal objects constructed with seams and joints is reflected in his teapots, jugs, storage jars and dishes.

Major exhibitions include: British Crafts Centre/Contemporary Applied Arts; Marianne Heller Gallery, Sandhausen; Crafts Council, Victoria and Albert Museum; Monmouth Museum; Freemantle Arts Centre, Australia; Westminster Gallery, Boston; Garth Clark Gallery, New York; Gryphon Gallery, Detroit; Candover Gallery, New Alresford.

Work represented in a number of collections in UK and overseas.

Colin Kellam

 K.

Born in 1942 in Leicestershire. Now lives in Devon. Colin Kellam trained at Loughborough College of Art, then worked for Marianne de Trey for five years until he opened his present workshop in 1967. He undertook a British Council Workshop Tour in India in 1984.

He works in stoneware making a range of domestic ware and employing six full time assistants in the workshop.

He does not take part in exhibitions, but his work is on sale at a number of galleries including: Amalgam, Barnes; Craftsmen Potters Association.

Dan Kelly

Born in 1953 in London where he still lives. Studied ceramics a Camberwell School of Arts and Crafts and the Royal College of A between 1973 and 1979. He has been involved in the setting up of variou workshops, and is undertaking a post-graduate teaching fellowship a Christ's Hospital, Sussex.

All his work is thrown, the larger pieces being made in sections. Whit and coloured slips are sometimes applied for surface detail and contras Large pieces have predominated in Dan Kelly's recent work. He i contemplating, in addition, pots of a different scale.

Major exhibitions include: Anatol Orient; Sussex University; Paul Ric Gallery; Christ's Hospital, Horsham; Artsite, Bath; Michaelson an Orient; Shape and Surface – touring exhibition.

Ruth King

Born in 1955 in Enfield, Middlesex. Lives in Yorkshire. Trained at Camberwell School of Arts and Crafts and from 1978 worked in London producing a range of coiled pots in simple forms. She moved to York in 1981 and to her present studio there in 1987.

She uses various stoneware clays either salt glazed in a wood fired kiln or oxidized to 1260°C. The pots are slab or coil built with impressed inlaid or applied decoration, coloured slips or glazes, depending on the firing method. The experimentation with salt glaze arose out of a dissatisfaction with her oxidized pieces. The adaptation of form and decoration led to gentler and more accessible pots all round, and currently both methods of firing are being used.

Major exhibitions include: Craftsmen Potters Association; New Ashgate Gallery, Farnham; British Crafts Centre/Contemporary Applied Arts; Scottish Gallery, Edinburgh; Grape Lane Gallery, York; Castle Museum, Nottingham; Norwich Castle Museum; Galerie de Vier Linden, Holland.

Julian King-Salter

Born in 1954 in Oldham. Lives in Dyfed. He has had no formal ar
training, but learned pottery under David Buchanan at Marlborougl
College. In 1983 he set up his pottery in Wales where he works full time.
Julian King-Salter's pots are stoneware, handbuilt by using flattenec
coils, followed by pinching. No further finish is given to the surface unti
glazes are applied to the biscuit pot by pouring and brushing. His pot:
are fired to 1260°C in an electric kiln.

Major exhibitions include: Welsh Arts Council; Amalgam, Barnes
Scottish Gallery; Leigh Gallery, London; New Ashgate Gallery, Farnham
Courcoux and Courcoux, Salisbury; Royal Exchange, Manchester.

Gabriele Koch

Born in 1948 in Lörrach, West Germany. Lives in London. After graduating in English at Heidelberg Gabriele Koch took up pottery at evening classes while teaching in London. A full time course at Goldsmiths' College followed and on leaving in 1981 she set up her own workshop. She is influenced by the Spanish landscape and folk pottery, by pots of early and primitive cultures. She uses principally porcelain. All pieces are coiled and covered with slip. They are repeatedly burnished before firing to 1000°C. In a second firing they are slowly smoked in sawdust. Some are raku fired.

Major exhibitions include: 1984 Biennale Internationale, Vallauris, France; British Crafts Centre/Contemporary Applied Arts; Amalgam, Barnes; Beaux Arts, Bath; Sheila Harrison Fine Art, London; Oxford Gallery; The Scottish Gallery; Bluecoat Display Centre, Liverpool; The Craft Centre and Design Gallery, Leeds; Art 16'85 Basle, Switzerland; Galerie Gilbert, Remetschweil, Germany.

91

Hilary Laforce

Born in 1957 in Suffolk. Lives in Warwickshire. Trained at West Surrey College of Art and Design, Farnham, then worked in a cooperative pottery workshop in Canada for a year. On returning to England she spent two years making tiles and architectural ceramics in a terra cotta workshop before setting up her own studio.

She uses red earthenware usually coil built and pinched, occasionally press moulded. The glazed surface is built up by multiple layers of colour and pattern using wax resist, lace templates, spraying and sponging. She is experimenting with wider ranges of textures and colours.

Major exhibitions include: Hiberna Gallery, Ottawa; Trinity Arts Centre, Tunbridge Wells; Design 88, San Francisco; The Minories, Colchester, Barbican Centre, London; Yew Tree Gallery, Gloucestershire; Oriel 31 Welshpool; Beaux Arts, Bath.

Peter Lane

Born in 1932 in Cairo. Now lives in Cumbria. Studied painting and ceramics at Bath Academy of Art. His extensive teaching experience in Art and Ceramics was pursued full time until 1984 when he decided to devote more time to his own work and writing. He still regularly undertakes lectures, workshops and exhibitions worldwide.

His work is mainly in porcelain, but also earthenware and stoneware. He makes principally thrown and turned vessel forms especially bowls and bottles. They are incised, carved, pierced or decorated by air brush with ceramic stains. His stimulus is a love of natural forms and landscapes, especially those of the Lake District.

Major exhibitions include: Casson Gallery, London; British Crafts Centre/Contemporary Applied Arts; The Scottish Gallery, Edinburgh; Rufford Craft Centre, Nottinghamshire; Craftsmen Potters Association; Galerie L, Hamburg; Westminster Gallery, Boston; Terranga Galerie, Dornbirn, Austria; Keramik Galerie Böwig, Hannover.

Work represented in many public collections in Britain and overseas.

Rodney Lawrence

Born in 1950 in London. Lives in Somerset. Trained at Harrow School of Art, followed by a short period with David Leach – a major influence on Rodney Lawrence's work. In 1976 he set up a pottery near Glastonbury with Elizabeth Raeburn. He teaches in Adult Education.

His work is stoneware – light buff and dark brown clay, thrown and turned. His decoration may be abstract or figurative, and he uses a variety of slip decorating methods. Pots are electric and wood fired to 1200°C.

Major exhibitions include: The Gallery, Newbury; Dan Klein, London; Bluecoat Display Centre, Liverpool; Hill Samuel, London; Southampton Art Gallery; Rural Life Museum, Somerset; Rufford Craft Centre, Nottinghamshire; Galerie Besson, London.

Bernard Leach

1887–1979. Born in Hong Kong. Studied under Tonks at the Slade School of Art. In Japan he attended a raku decorating party and turned to pottery, studying under Ogata Kenzan. He returned to England in 1920 with Shoji Hamada and set up his workshop at St Ives on traditional Japanese lines. A series of pupils arrived beginning with Michael Cardew, Katharine Pleydell Bouverie and Norah Braden. In the 1930s Leach built a kiln at Dartington Hall at the invitation of the Elmhirsts, sympathetic to the educational reforms they were introducing. In the 1940s Leach's most influential work, *A Potter's Book,* was published, leading to lecture tours in th USA. He returned many times to Japan. His sight failing, in 1972 he ceased potting.

His early work was slipware, the majority of his pieces stoneware and porcelain decorated generally by means of wax resist, sgraffito or brushwork. Undeniably the most influential British potter of this century, he is as famous in Japan and the East as in Europe and America.

Exhibited in London at the Little Gallery, Beaux Arts Gallery, and Primavera. His work is represented world-wide in many public collections.

David Leach

Born in 1911 in Tokyo, arriving at St Ives in 1920 with his parents and Hamada. On leaving school he worked in the pottery at Dartington Hall. After a technical course at North Staffordshire College he returned to St Ives, establishing a range of stoneware and stayed there, with the exception of the war years, until the 1950s. In 1955 he moved to his own pottery at Lowerdown, Bovey Tracey, Devon where he still lives. He made slipware only there until 1961. He now produces porcelain and stoneware individual and domestic pieces. Fluted shapes are a particular hallmark. Almost all his work is thrown, and decoration may be carved, wax resist, combed, sgraffito or painted. He has developed his own glazes. Teaching at Loughborough and other schools has been an important part of David Leach's career.

Major exhibitions include: Craftsmen Potters Association; International Academy of Ceramics, Istanbul; Kettles Yard, Cambridge; Decorative Art Museum, Copenhagen; Somers Gallery, Heidelberg; New Ashgate Gallery, Farnham; Peter Dingley, Stratford-upon-Avon; British Crafts Centre/Contemporary Applied Arts.

Work represented in many public collections in the UK and overseas.

96

Janet Leach

Born in Texas in 1918. In 1947 she became interested in pottery. After training she visited Japan to study at Hamada's pottery, and the mountain village Tamba. She was the first western woman to study pottery in Japan. She moved to England to marry Bernard Leach and now runs the Leach Pottery. She works in a variety of clays with shapes and forms from the Japanese tradition. Most of her work is thrown on the wheel, then may be dented, slashed or scored. Some is slab built. All is strong and powerful. Slash marks on her pots are made with glaze. On some pieces she uses a friable wood ash which is fired to a liquid state and trickles down the pot to make its own pattern. Other freely thrown pots are fired amongst the wood, taking on all the effects of the firing.

Major exhibitions include: Primavera, London; Sheila Harrison Fine Art; Crafts Council; Kettles Yard, Cambridge; British Crafts Centre/ Contemporary Applied Arts; Amalgam, Barnes; Boymans Museum, Rotterdam; Paul Rice Gallery, London; Diamaru Department Store, Japan; Takashimaya Department Store, Japan.

Work represented in public collections in UK, USA, Japan, Denmark, Holland.

John Leach

Born in 1939 at Pottery Cottage, St Ives, son of David Leach, grandson o
Bernard. No formal art school training. John undertook a five yeaı
apprenticeship with his father which included periods with Ray Finch
Colin Pearson and Bernard Leach. After his apprenticeship he took up ;
teaching post in California and helped to establish Mendocino Pottery
He returned to England to begin Muchelney Pottery in Somerset in 1964
The pottery produces a standard range of kitchen woodfired stoneware
and John Leach makes individual pieces too, which show an African
influence since his study tour in Nigeria in 1984. His pieces are thrown
by hand, and are developing simpler forms with less complicatec
decoration. He undertakes extensive workshop tours of Canada, USA.

Major exhibitions include: Leach Family, Japan 1980; One man -
Parnham House, Dorset; Makers Eye Crafts Council; Peter Dingley
Stratford-upon-Avon; New Ashgate Gallery, Farnham; Hanley Museum
Stoke; Rufford Craft Centre, Nottingham; Hobro, Denmark; Greenwicl
House, New York.

Jennifer Lee

Born in 1956 in Aberdeenshire. Now lives in London. Studied ceramics at Edinburgh College of Art and Royal College of Art. In between she spent six months in the USA visiting leading potters in California, Washington and Oregon. She set up her studio in London in 1983. Her pots are handbuilt using coil and pinch methods. The stoneware clay is coloured by the addition of oxides, body stains and underglaze, rather than surface glazes or slips. The pots are burnished and once fired between 1200 and 1270°C.

Major exhibitions include: Scottish Gallery, Edinburgh; Anatol Orient, London; Crafts Council, Victoria and Albert Museum; Amalgam, Barnes; Queensberry Hunt Studio, London; Beaux Arts, Bath; Marianne Heller Galerie, Sandhausen; Osaka and Tokyo, New British Design; Craft and Folk Museum, Los Angeles.

Work represented in many public collections in UK and overseas.

Eileen Lewenstein

Born in 1925. Now lives in Brighton, East Sussex. After training as a painter she came across pottery by chance during an art teacher's Diploma course. She was greatly helped by Bob Washington's teaching at Derby School of Art. She formed the Briglin Pottery in London with Brigitta Appleby and from 1948 to 1958 produced repetition ware before beginning her career as an individual potter.

She was a lecturer in ceramics at Hornsey from 1960 until 1969, and has been a co-editor of *Ceramics Review* for eighteen years.

Eileen Lewenstein works in stoneware and porcelain by throwing, coiling and press moulding techniques. Her pots and sculptures develop separately, the latter being currently influenced by her nearby beach.

Major exhibitions include: Kettles Yard, Cambridge, Craftsmen Potters Association; Fitzwilliam Museum, Cambridge; New Ashgate Gallery, Farnham; Crafts Council, London; Vallauris – New York, New Zealand, Sydney.

Work included in many public and private collections in UK and overseas.

Gillian Lowndes

No mark used

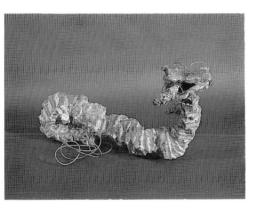

Born in 1936, she spent her childhood in India. Studied at the Central School of Arts and Crafts. She shared a workshop with Robin Welch in Bloomsbury concentrating on a wide variety of hand-built work. She found the technical limitations tedious. A two year stay in Nigeria with her husband Ian Auld was a turning point. On return she developed wider technqiues using other materials, for example fibreglass dipped in slip which made porcelain bags containing bricks and held together with wire; broken cups, chair springs and steel all coated with sand to produce granular surfaces. Some elements are painted and spotted with oxides and under-glaze colours. The only limitation on the materials she uses is the effect of the firing process on them.

Major exhibitions include: Primavera, London and Cambridge; Crafts Council Gallery; British Crafts Centre/Contemporary Applied Arts; Sunderland Arts Centre Touring Exhibition; Amalgam, Barnes; British Ceramics, Scharpoord, Knokke-Heist, Belgium; Fitzwilliam Museum, Cambridge; Gardner Centre Gallery, Brighton.

Work represented in many public collections in UK and USA.

101

Jim Malone

Born in 1946 in Sheffield. Now lives in Cumbria. Trained at Camberwell School of Art in the early 1970s, and worked from a studio in Wales until 1982, when he became a full time lecturer at Cumbria College of Art, Carlisle. Now setting up a new workshop in Cumbria.

His work is mostly stoneware, thrown on an oriental type kick wheel. Decoration is usually engraved, but he uses some brush decoration either in the form of wax resist or over a background of hakeme slip. All work is functional.

Exhibitions have been numerous both in Britian, USA and the Far East.

Work in public collections includes: Victoria and Albert Museum; Paisley Museum, Glasgow; Merseyside Museum and Art Gallery; Milner White Collection, York; Bolton Museum and Art Gallery.

Kate Malone

Born in 1959 in London, where she still lives. Studied at Bristol Polytechnic under Mo Jupp, Nick Homoky, Wally Keeler and George Rayner, and at the Royal College of Art under David Hamilton. Recent travels to Egypt, India, USA, Thailand and Mexico have been an influence on her work alongside an appreciation of the techniques of traditional English ceramics, and a constant search for new effects to apply to new forms. She works in various clays, using many different methods. Pieces may have up to ten firings to build up a glossy depth of colour which runs in streams over a pot. With a new large kiln she intends to make some larger architectural pieces. Working on a number of commissions for tile and wall panels and etched glass.

Major exhibitions include: Contemporary Applied Arts; Young Breed, The Barbican, London; Jugend Gestaltet, Munich; Chicago (Crafts Council representative) Freuds Gallery, London; Hannah Peschar Gallery, Ockford; The Orangery, Holland Park, London; RCA Retrospective, Kyoto; Manchester City Art Gallery.

John Maltby

Born in Lincolnshire. Now living in Devon. He studied sculpture at Leicester and Goldsmiths' College and taught painting and sculpture for two and a half years before joining David Leach at Bovey Tracey. In 1964 he started his own pottery at Stoneshill in Devon, making stoneware, earthenware and porcelain. He now makes only individual pots, usually vessels in stoneware, and often decorated with enamels. They may be decorated in light colours on one side, dark on the other, illustrating day and night. He lectures widely in England and overseas, particularly Norway.

Major exhibitions include: Amalgam, Barnes; New Ashgate Gallery Farnham; Oxford Gallery; Westminster Gallery, Boston; Beaux Arts Bath; Peter Dingley, Stratford-upon-Avon; Siebu, Tokyo; Victoria and Albert Museum; Craftsmen Potters Association.

Work represented in many museums and public collections.

Imogen Margrie

Born in 1962 in London where she still lives. Trained at Colchester
Institute and Central School of Art, with Eileen Nisbet, Gordon Baldwin
and Gillian Lowndes as tutors. Major influences include Mexican
ceramics, Elizabeth Frink, Brancusi, and Rodin.

She works in stoneware, making figurative ceramics, principally birds.
All pieces are coiled, decorated with engobes and fired to 1200°C, fired
again with more underglazes, and finally decorated with enamels.

Major exhibitions include: Chelsea Crafts Fair; British Crafts Centre/
Contemporary Applied Arts; Oxford Gallery; Leigh Gallery, London;
Casson Gallery, London; Kingsgate Workshops; Scottish Gallery,
Edinburgh; Anatol Orient, London; Ladygate Gallery, Yorkshire.

William Marshall

Born in 1923. Lives in St Ives in Cornwall. The first apprentice to be employed at the Leach Pottery in 1938, he remained there until Bernard Leach's death, often producing pots for him to decorate. Leach said of him in 1978 'he has gradually become quite an expressive potter – one of the best in the country. Now in my old age he has been my right hand man.' Since Leach's death in 1979 William Marshall has set up his own studio producing pots in the Leach tradition. He exhibited with Bernard Leach at Libertys in 1956, at Primavera and in Rotterdam.

Other exhibitions include: Christopher Wood Gallery; O'Casey's Craft Gallery, London; Amalgam, Barnes.

Andrew McGarva

Born in 1956 and spent his childhood in Scotland. Now lives in Hereford and Worcester. Worked part time for Michael and Sheila Casson before studying at West Surrey College of Art and Design. Six months in a pottery village in France was a strong influence on his early work. On leaving college he set up his own workshop. Between 1980 and 1987 he taught beginners, students and professionals, and worked as adviser to a pottery project in India. Ceased Art School teaching in 1987 to concentrate on production and design work. He has always made functional stoneware, usually thrown on the wheel. Early decoration was mainly slip trailed or modelled, and pieces wood fired or salt glazed. More recently he has become known for his brush decoration.

Major exhibitions include: Craft Study Centre, Bath; British Crafts Centre/Contemporary Applied Arts; Liverpool Garden Festival; Aberystwyth Arts Centre; Melrose Station Arts Centre, Scotland; Ten years at Wobage Farm.

Overseas exhibitions in Japan, West Germany and the USA.

Carol McNicoll

Born in 1943 in Birmingham. Lives in London. Studied at Leeds Polytechnic and Royal College of Art. She makes tableware, vases, etc which remain vessels although unconventional ones not intended for practical use. Her work is hand-built and often elaborate in construction imitating in clay other materials such as cloth, weaving or knitting. She enjoys awkward shapes and makes models in paper or card before constructing each pot. Slabs of white earthenware are coloured and patterned before being assembled. Moulds may be used for some of the component parts. Further decoration is sprayed and stencilled and firing and refiring continue until the desired effect is achieved.

Major exhibitions include: Thumb Gallery London; Axis, Paris; Galerie het Kapelhuis, Amersfoort, Holland; Knokke-Heist, Belgium; Aspects London; Crafts Council, London; Francis Kyle, London; Crafts Council Victoria and Albert Museum.

Peter Meanley

pm88

Born in 1944 in Huddersfield. Now lives in County Down and responsible for the Ceramics Course at the University of Ulster. Trained at York School of Art and the Royal College of Art. For the past few years Peter Meanley has been working to rediscover qualities which characterized Thomas Whieldon and other fine English potters of the late 18th and early 19th centuries. Currently he makes salt glazed teapots, only about 25 per year, and would like to mount an exhbition in 3–5 years' time to demonstrate a new tradition of salt glazed teapot making.

He works in stoneware, throwing, turning, press moulding, painting with slips, and waxing, before firing at about 1000°C.

Major exhibitions include: Craftsmen Potters Association; Arts Council of Northern Ireland, Belfast; Rufford Craft Centre, Nottingham; Galerie L, Hamburg; Marie Jordan Gallery, Wakefield; Irish Crafts Council; Contemporary Applied Arts.

Eric James Mellon

Born in 1925 in Hertfordshire. Lives in West Sussex. Studied at Watford Harrow and the Central School of Arts and Crafts. He has carried ou many technical experiments over the years on the firing of colours anc pigments in conjunction with tree and bush ash glazes. He works ir stoneware and some porcelain and intricately decorates his pieces with figurative brush drawn decoration, on themes ranging from mythology tc personal symbolism and social comment. The fox which appears with the signature on each piece is a Japanese good-luck symbol for the kilr firing.

Major exhibitions include: Primavera, London and Cambridge; Victoria and Albert Museum; Seibu Store, Tokyo; Contemporary Applied Arts London; Craftsmen Potters Association; Westminster Gallery, Boston Paul Rice Gallery, London; Courcoux & Courcoux, Salisbury; Galeric Terranga, Dornbirn, Austria.

Work in a number of public collections in Great Britain and overseas.

Jon Middlemiss

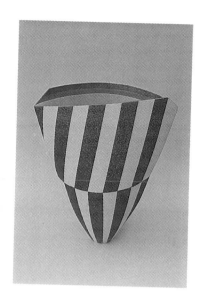

Born in 1949 in Harrogate. Now lives in Cornwall. Studied painting and print making at Scarborough and Exeter Colleges of Art, and made extensive trips to Europe and the Middle East studying geometry and pattern in mosaics and architecture. Self taught as a potter, he set up workshops in Devon making functional ware before moving to Cornwall in 1980 where he began to make individual pieces.

His work is thrown and hand-built, cut, carved and extensively worked on. A wide range of glazes lustres and semi precious stones are used to create various surfaces, textures and colours. He is developing further interest in the symbolism of form, and the balance between geometry and assymetry, influenced by recent travels to New Mexico and Arizona.

Major exhibitions include: Amalgam, Barnes; Salthouse Gallery, St Ives; Scottish Gallery, Edinburgh; Beaux Arts, Bath; Elaine Potter, San Francisco; Freehand Gallery, Los Angeles.

Ursula Mommens

Born in 1908 in Cambridge. Lives in Sussex. In her own words, she spent two wasted years at the Central School, then a year at the Royal College of Art under Staite Murray exploring the V & A! She began working on her own in a cowhouse in Kent using an old flower pot wheel and oil engine and a small oil kiln. From 1935 she worked in London with her husband Julian Trevelyan until her kiln was blitzed, when she had the opportunity to join Michael Cardew at Winchcombe and Wenford Bridge. She works principally in stoneware thrown on the wheel, using chiefly a tenmoku glaze of her own, though she has started to use porcelain which has led to some new shapes and decoration. She makes a range of domestic ware to be sold as cheaply as possible, plus individual pieces.

Major exhibitions include: Primavera, London; New Ashgate Gallery, Farnham; Rye Art Gallery; Henry Rothschild Selection, Kettles Yard, Cambridge; Southover Gallery, Lewes; Michael Cardew and friends; Craftsmen Potters Association; Terrace Gallery, Worthing; Galerie Besson, London.

Work represented in a number of public collections in UK.

Denis Moore

1908–1977. Lived at East Horsley, Surrey. Self taught, he gave up a legal career at 40 to become a potter. For more than twenty years he worked in high fired stoneware, using local raw materials. He developed a wide range of copper and ash glazes, using an open fired kiln fuelled with wood and oil. He was inspired by Chinese and Japanese pottery. Denis Moore exhibited at the Craftsmen Potters Association and Primavera, in the 1960s and Guildford House in the 1960s and 1970s.

His work can be seen in collections at the Victoria and Albert Museum and Sudbury Hall.

William Staite Murray

1881–1962. Born in Deptford. His family were much opposed to any interest in art and it was not until about 1909 that Straite Murray enrolled at Camberwell and extended his interest in painting into the field of pottery. In 1919 he set up a studio to make high fired stoneware in the manner of Sung pottery. Leach and Hamada exchanged views and advice with him. He exhibited in 1923 at the Leicester Galleries, and subsequently with the Arts League of Service. His first one man show was at Paterson's Gallery in Old Bond Street. He aspired to gain acceptance for pottery on the same terms as fine art and put high prices on his work. His appointment as Head of the Pottery School at the Royal College of Art led to a breakdown in relations between him and Leach. Gradually he had been decorating an increasing number of pots with brushwork, incising, or inlay, and figurative designs followed. His reliance on the Chinese style disappeared and collectors of paintings sought his work. He enjoyed a considerable period of popularity in the late 1920s and early 1930s. The Murrays were in Rhodesia visiting relatives when the war broke out. There they remained and died.

Excellent examples of Straite Murray's work are in the Milner White collection at York and Southampton Art Galleries.

Bryan Newman

Born in 1935 in London. Lives in Somerset. He trained at Camberwell School of Art in the 1950s and subsequently taught there and at Bath Academy of Art when he moved his pottery to Somerset. He gave up teaching in 1973. He makes a range of thrown domestic stoneware at Aller Pottery, and also distinctive sculptural pieces which are assembled from thrown and slabbed units into intricate forms, boats, buildings, housescapes and bridges. He has travelled widely overseas, giving pottery workshops demonstrations and visiting countries where pottery remains part of the folk tradition. He prefers to exhibit in group ceramic shows rather than in gallery solo exhibitions.

Major exhibitions include: Primavera 1964; Peter Dingley, Stratford-upon-Avon; Craftsmen Potters Association; Overseas exhibitions in Munich, Hamburg, Geneva, Copenhagen, Tokyo, San Francisco, Sydney and Melbourne.

Work represented in the collections of the Victoria and Albert and Inner London Education Authority.

Eileen Nisbet

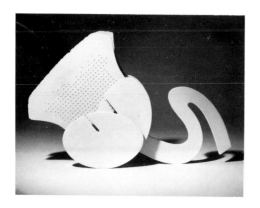

Born in London in 1929. Lives in London. Studied at the Central School
of Art and Design, and has taught subsequently at Harrow and Central
School. Until the late 1970s she made earthenware and stoneware dishes
and panels. She now works in porcelain or with firing clay, making
fragile sculptural pieces about movement and balance. Thin rolled slabs
are dried and fired extremely slowly to prevent warping, and then shaped
and assembled. Sometimes the edges are broken away, resembling slate,
others are smooth and flat. They are inlaid and painted with slips and
enamels using a restricted colour range, and joined by tubular porcelain
sections. Some forms suggest vessels, others aeroplanes and clouds.

Exhibitions include: Contemporary Applied Arts; Casson Gallery,
London; Craftsmen Potters Association; Beaux Arts, Bath; Maya Behn
Gallery, Zurich; Crafts Council; Graham Gallery, New York; Westminster
Gallery, Boston; Knokke-Heist, Belgium.

Work represented in a number of public collections in the UK and
overseas.

Born in 1958 in Swansea. Now living on the Gower, West Glamorgan. Trained at Bath Academy of Art. In 1984 set up a joint ceramic workshop with her sister Sarah. Her work is usually raku and figurative. Her main influences are the serenity of T'ang Dynasty earthenware figures and horses and at the same time the colour and vitality of fairground and circus animals and folk art.

She uses a mixture of different clays raku fired between 1000 and 1020°C. The animals are constructed with a combination of slabs, press moulds and modelling. The surfaces are part glazed, part unglazed.

Major exhibitions include: Touring exhibition with The Northern Centre for Contemporary Art, Sunderland; Parnham House, Dorset; Beaux Arts, Bath; Amalgam, Barnes; Peter Dingley, Stratford-upon-Avon; Oxford Gallery; Ladygate Gallery, Beverley; Courcoux and Courcoux, Salisbury.

Sarah Noël

Born in 1961 in Mumbles, Swansea. Lives on the Gower, Wes
Glamorgan. Trained at Bristol Polytechnic, and in 1984 set up a join
workshop with her sister, Anna. Her work, like that of her sister, is rak
and figurative. Her main influences are the theatre – from stage sets t
posing figures; medieval drawings and religious icons and the boat
sailors and seagulls of the Swansea docks.

She uses a mixture of clays raku fired between 1000 and 1020°C. Eac
piece is made up of two slabs of clay on which the design is drawn wit
a knife. Smoky unglazed areas contrast with colourful glazed areas.

Major exhibitions include: Newport Art Gallery, South Wales; Staffor
City Art Gallery; Oriel 31, Welshpool; Beaux Arts, Bath; Amalgam
Barnes; Peter Dingley, Stratford-upon-Avon; Ladygate Gallery, Beverley
Ayling Porteous, Chester; Higher Street Gallery, Dartmouth; Courcou
and Courcoux, Salisbury.

Magdalene Odundo

Odundo
1988

Born in Kenya. Lives in Hampshire. Trained at Cambridge and West Surrey Colleges of Art with periods at the Abuja Pottery in Nigeria and teaching at the Commonwealth Institute, London, before undertaking her MA at the Royal College of Art.

Her pots are vessels concerned with space and form, and with little embellishment. They are handbuilt by coiling, finished with a clay slip, and smoothed and burnished before and after the slip is applied. Various firing processes produce the range of rust, orange and lustrous black finishes.

Major exhibitions include: Africa Centre, London; Crafts Council; Craftsmen Potters Association; Hot House, New York; Bluecoat Display Centre, Liverpool; Queensburry Hunt Studio, London; Courcoux and Courcoux, Salisbury; Anne Berthoud Gallery, London; Beaux Arts, Bath.

Work included in public collections in Great Britain and overseas.

Jane Osborn-Smith

Born in 1952. Lives in New York. Studied ceramics at Hornsey and Royal College of Art. In 1977 joined 401½ workshop studio in London. Has worked as a freelance designer for Rosenthal Studio Line, Germany, and for Steuben Glass, New York.

Her pieces are made of porcelain and parian, slip cast or slab built, then high fired and finished in a variety of ways, by burnishing, polishing or fume glazing, and painted with under-glaze enamels or lustres.

Major exhibitions include: Christopher Wood Gallery, London; British Craft Centre/Contemporary Applied Arts; Bohun Gallery, Henley-on-Thames; Makers Eye, Crafts Council; Westminster Gallery, Boston; Queensberry Hunt Studio, London; Crafts Alliance Gallery, St Louis; Rockwell Museum, Corning.

Elspeth Owen

Born in 1938 in Buckinghamshire, now lives in Cambridgeshire. She is self taught after working as a historian, teacher and counsellor, and approached clay initially in the context of therapy. She is a tutor for the Open University. Aspects of life which have influenced her work include the west coasts of the British Isles, the women's movement, the Greenham Common Women's Peace Camp, walking and dancing.

Elspeth Owen makes low temperature burnished pots in a wide range of clays, by pinching and slab building. The differing coloured clays form the principal decoration, enhanced by smoked areas and resist patterns.

Major exhibitions include: Scottish Gallery, Edinburgh; Fitzwilliam Museum, Cambridge; Kettles Yard, Cambridge; Crafts Council, Victoria and Albert Museum; Leeds City Art Gallery; New Craftsman, St Ives; Hamburg Museum, West Germany; Aberystwyth Arts Centre, Wales.

Work included in a number of public collections.

Mabel Padfield

Born in 1938 in Cheshire. Now lives in West Sussex. After a Scienc
degree at Bristol, she began to teach children with special needs, at th
same time developing her interest in painting and drawing. In 1979 sh
became ceramic assistant to Eric James Mellon and continues to wor
with him.

Her stoneware pots are thrown and decorated with oxides using bus
ash glazes, particularly from Escallonia. Decorations used are studies o
fish and plant forms. Pots are fired in a gas kiln to 1280 to 1300°C. Ne
glazes from straw and peat ash are being developed.

Major exhibitions include: David Paul Gallery, Chichester; Departmen
of Energy, London; Godfrey & Twatt, Harrogate.

Colin Pearson

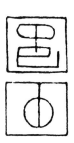

Born in 1923 in London. Lives in London. After the war he studied painting at Goldsmiths' College then worked at Winchcombe Pottery under Ray Finch and at David Leach's Aylesford Pottery. In 1961 he set up his own pottery, making individual pieces in porcelain and stoneware. He teaches part time at Camberwell School of Art.

He works in stoneware and porcelain making vessels with 'wings'. His pieces are thrown, then altered sometimes to a rectangular or oval shape before the wings are added.

Major exhibitions include: Craftsmen Potters Association, London; Oxford Gallery; Gallery 77 Belgrade, Yugoslavia; Beaux Arts, Bath; Amalgam, Barnes; Crafts Council; Darmstadt Museum, Germany.

Frequent exhibitions in Europe, USA and Japan. Work represented in a number of public collections in UK and overseas.

Roger Perkins

No mark use

Born in 1952 in London. Now lives in Oxford. Trained at Camberwe
School of Arts and Crafts. Artist in residence at the University c
Delaware USA in 1984. He now teaches at several schools in Oxfordshir
and lectures at various colleges.

He works in clay, wood, stone and metal, combining handbuilding c
clay with other materials. Clay is used as part of the sculpting process a
a sculptural material rather than as a vessel, though his early work i
clay was often in vessel form.

Major exhibitions include: Woodstock Museum, Oxfordshire; Dan Klei
London; Oxford Gallery; Galerie Gilbert, Remetschwiel, German
University of Delaware; Galerie Septentrion, France.

Gwyn Hanssen Pigott

No mark used

Born in 1935 in Australia. Trained there and with Ray Finch, Bernard Leach and Michael Cardew in England. In 1959 she married Louis Hanssen and they set up a pottery in London making tableware and exhibiting in group and solo exhibitions. After her husband's death Gwyn Hanssen attended classes by Lucie Rie at Camberwell, and ran Cardew's pottery while he was away in Africa before setting up a pottery in central France to make woodfired tableware. In 1973 she returned to Australia where she produces porcelain and stoneware tableware and industrial pieces. She has always been heavily involved in teaching, and is presently Craftsman in residence at Brisbane College of Adult Education.

Major exhibitions include: Primavera, London; Libertys; British Craft Centre; Victor Mace Fine Art Gallery, Brisbane; Casson Gallery, London; Blackfriars Gallery, Sydney.

Work represented in public collections in UK and overseas.

Henry Pim

Born in 1947 in Sussex. Lives in London. Trained at Camberwell School of Arts and Crafts.

He makes large pots in earthenware and stoneware with richly mottled glazes. The clay is rolled out and the surface impressed with a decorated texture before the pot is assembled. There is little working of the clay after assembly because this would damage the surface. The slabs are seamed together and a range of slips and glazes applied by brush, trailer or pouring. Henry Pim cannot pinpoint the origin of his influences but he reads about African, South American and early European artefacts.

Major exhibitions include: Aspects, London; Contemporary Applied Arts; Crafts Council; Anatol Orient, London; Galerie L, Hamburg; European Crafts Today, Tokyo and Osaka; Garth Clark Gallery, New York and Kansas City; Solomon Gallery, Dublin; Aberystwyth Arts Centre.

126

Helen Pincombe

Born in 1908 in India and educated in Australia. She arrived in England at the age of 17. Studied at Camberwell, Central School and the Royal College of Art, teaching at the Royal College during the war when it moved to Ambleside.

After the war she established a pottery at Oxshott, Surrey near to that of Denise Wren, potting firstly part time and later full time. She is best known for her stoneware bowls and range of high temperature glazes.

Exhibitions: Primavera and various others in UK and abroad.

Work represented in museums in UK and abroad.

Ian Pirie

Born in 1951 in Fraserburgh. Now lives in Stonehaven. Trained at Grays School of Art, Aberdeen. Set up a joint pottery in Aberdeen in 1975, initially making domestic ware. He now teaches full time on the Ceramics Degree Course at Aberdeen.

He works mainly in high fired porcelain. Surface decoration is an important element in all Ian Pirie's pieces. Earlier pieces may have linear black incisions or printed transfers. More recent pots have airbrush and hand drawn decoration, and there is an increasing emphasis on the three dimensional form.

Major exhibitions include: Scottish Craft Centre, Edinburgh; National Museum of Wales; Craftsmen Potters Association; The Chestnut Gallery, Bourton-on-the-Water; Keramik Galerie Bowig, Hannover; Rufford Crafts Centre; Freemantle Arts Centre, Australia.

Work exhibited in a number of public collections in UK.

John Pollex

Born in 1941 in Huntingdon. Lives in Plymouth. Trained at Harrow College of Art then worked as assistant to Bryan Newman and Colin Pearson. Established his present workshop in 1971. He is a part time lecturer at Medway College of Design in Kent and regularly undertakes seminars and demonstrations in Britain and overseas.

In the 1970s and early 1980s he produced traditional slipware in the style of Thomas Toft. Since 1984, having developed a range of coloured slips, his decoration has become more individual. Recent work has been influenced by the paintings of Patrick Heron and Howard Hodgkin. He works in red earthenware applying coloured slips with brushes and sponges, as well as trailing and sgraffito. He is working towards larger works for hanging, as opposed to domestic use.

Major exhibitions include: Simon Drew Gallery, Dartmouth; Innate Harmony, London; Bluecoat Display Centre, Liverpool; Craftsmen Potters Association; Victoria and Albert Museum; Stoke-on-Trent Museum and Art Gallery.

Jacqui Poncelet

Born in 1947 in Belgium, she has lived in the UK since the age of four. Studied at Wolverhampton College of Art and the Royal College of Art. Shared a studio with Glenys Barton and Alison Britton.

In the 1970s she worked in bone china with pierced or stained surfaces. The pieces were first cast, then carved. In 1977 she abandoned bone china for the freedom of slab built forms in stoneware and earthenware with bold colours and patterns. Her 1980s work shows pot forms ousted by organic forms, horns, claws, spikes, etc, made by grafting together separately made hollow elements. Some are coiled, most moulded, and they are decorated with various colours of slip and glaze.

Major exhibitions include: Crafts Council; Graham Gallery, New York; British Council tour – Australia and New Zealand; Museum of Art, Pennsylvania State University; Amalgam, Barnes; Whitechapel Art Gallery; Westminster Gallery, Boston; Craft Gallery, Japan.

Work included in numerous public collections in UK and overseas.

Rosa Quy

Born in 1960 in London where she still lives. Studied 3-Dimensional Design at Middlesex Polytechnic, and Ceramics at the Royal College of Art. Set up her workshop at 401½ Studios in 1987. Her influences are Chinese and Japanese ceramic sculpture. Her sculptures are coiled and raku fired. Her drawings on plates are stained with slips and oxides and fired up to five or six times. She is aiming to make her animal sculptures simpler and stronger in form in the future, perhaps more abstract. She is also decorating hand made tiles.

Exhibitions include: Anatol Orient; Sothebys Applied Art Show.

Sara Radstone

No mark used

Born in 1955 in London. Studied at Herefordshire College of Art and Camberwell, before setting up studios at 401½ workshops, and then Brixton. Her work is hand-built stoneware, with thin coils or slabs made from broken up leather hard pots. Her imagery comes from signs of disuse and damage, scratches, random marks, worn paint and aged surfaces. She wants her pots to seem to be on the verge of falling apart. The slight sparkle achieved by adding lithium carbonate is important to the surface. She is striving for more toughness. Oxides are often used to darken the markings, or a porcelain slip to make them prominent. One glaze is applied thickly, leaving some matt body surface.

Major exhibitions include: Amalgam, Barnes; Bohun Gallery, Henley on Thames; Crafts Council, Victoria and Albert Museum, London; Paul Rice Gallery, London; Anatol Orient, London; Westminster Gallery, Boston, British Council touring exhibition of Czechoslovakia.

132

Elizabeth Raeburn

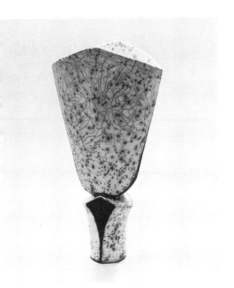

Born in 1943 in Surrey. Lives in Somerset. After working in music, book publishing and teaching she studied studio pottery at Harrow School of Art from 1973 to 1975. In 1975 she moved to her present studio in a converted chapel near Glastonbury. She works in stoneware, hand-building, and decorating with white or coloured slips before the first firing. After glazing, pots are raku fired in a gas or electric kiln between 900 and 1000°C. Woodshavings, sawdust or damp newspapers are used for the post firing reduction depending on the required effect.

Major exhibitions include: Dan Klein, London; Museum for Modern Ceramics, Deidesheim, Germany; Henry Rothschild's Choice, Zenith Gallery, Nottingham; Fischer Fine Art, London; Oxford Gallery; Galerie fur Keramik und Kalligraphic, Hamburg; Scottish Gallery, Edinburgh; Candover Gallery, New Alresford; Galerie Besson, London.

133

George Rainer

Born in 1923 in South China. Now lives near Bath. Worked as an artist in Australia before coming to England in 1948. Studied pottery at Camberwell School of Art, and subsequently Stoke-on-Trent. Established the Department of Ceramics at the West of England College of Art, later Bristol Polytechnic. A former chairman of The Craftsmen Potters Association. George Rainer, now retired, spends his time painting and drawing – mainly landscapes in the West Country. His pots are stoneware, hand-built and sculptural, and by preference retaining the hollow form. Not potting at present, George Rainer expects, if he pots again, to make thrown wares with simple painted decoration. Admiring a straightforward technique he now considers hand-building too fussy.

A number of exhibitions including Primavera, Cambridge, but principally at the Craftsmen Potters Association.

Stanislas Reychan

Born in 1897 in Vienna, of a Polish father and Austrian mother. His foreign language skills brought him to London during the war as Military Secretary to the Chief of the Polish General Staff. Here he found an interest in modelling and was helped at St Martin's by Walter Marsden, and at the Central School by Dora Billington, who taught him pottery. He opened a studio and managed from the beginning to support himself by the sale of his work. In the 1950s he exhibited regularly at the Royal Academy, and was awarded a silver medal at the Paris Salon in 1960.

Stanislas Reychan closed his workshop on his 88th birthday in 1985. He still lives in London.

Mary Rich

In the early 1960s she worked with David Leach and Harry and May Davis. She started her own workshop in 1962 and moved in 1970 to Cornwall, where she made mostly domestic stoneware. She now works entirely in porcelain. Her forms are simple and small – boxes, bowls, vases, with a rich surface texture and decoration of gold and other metals combined with coloured lustres. All pots are once fired in an oilfired kiln.

Major exhibitions include: Peter Dingley, Stratford-upon-Avon; Kettles Yard; Cambridge; Primavera, Cambridge; Craftsmen Potters Association; The English Gallery, Geinsenheim; Martha Schneider Gallery, Illinois; Westminster Gallery, Boston; Chestnut Gallery, Bourton-on-the-Water.

Christine-Ann Richards

Born in 1944 in Buckinghamshire. Lives in London. After training at Harrow School of Art and Technology under Mick Casson she worked for Bryan and Julia Newman and David Leach before starting her own workshop. A trip to China in 1978 radically affected her work. Of late she has begun to view her ceramics as canvases. Decoration has become calligraphic in her black and white pots.

She works in thrown porcelain, firing to 1260 to 1290°C. Earlier pots have matt glazes, more recent pieces have crackle glazes, sometimes plain, or stained with Chinese ink.

Major exhibitions include: Craftsmen Potters Association; Falcon House Gallery, Boxford; Galerie An Gross St Martin, Cologne; Victoria and Albert Museum, London; Terrace Gallery, Worthing; New Ashgate Gallery, Farnham; Amalgam, Barnes; St James' Gallery, Bath.

Lucie Rie

Born in 1902 in Vienna. Studied at the Vienna Kunstgewerbe Schule where the pottery style was rich and ornate. She came to England in 1938, establishing her workshop in London and after the war she made ceramic buttons and jewellery to meet post war need, before turning initially to functional pottery. Hans Coper, who had joined her as an assistant, worked with her on developing different forms. In 1950 they began to exhibit together at the Berkeley Galleries, and exhibitions overseas, including New York followed. In 1960 Lucie Rie began teaching at Camberwell School of Art. Recognition has grown over the years and Lucie Rie still pots full time.

Her work before 1948 was earthenware. Since then she has produced stoneware and porcelain. All her pots are thrown on the wheel and turned while leatherhard, the surface smoothed to remove throwing rings. Bottles are thrown in sections and returned to the wheel to be joined. Lucie Rie continues to explore different forms, new glazes and surfaces. Decoration is restrained, the most familiar being the incised lines scratched on the rough slip with a pin. Glaze is applied by brush, and pots are once fired only.

Lucie Rie has exhibited worldwide and her work is represented in public collections in the UK and overseas.

David Roberts

Born in 1947 in Sheffield. Now lives in Huddersfield. Introduced to ceramics during a degree course at Bretton Hall College, Yorkshire. While a full time art teacher he became increasingly involved in making pots. In 1981 he gave up full time teaching to concentrate on pot making and is now one of a small number of British potters specialising in raku. He is visiting lecturer at Dewsbury College and holds a number of workshops throughout the country.

He makes large coil built raku-fired pots, usually bottles and bowls. He is concerned with simplicity of form and the control of surface which arises from the firing and reduction process.

Major exhibitions include: Beaux Arts, Bath; British Crafts Centre/ Contemporary Applied Arts; Westminster Gallery, Boston; Scottish Gallery, Edinburgh; Aberystwyth Arts Centre; Courcoux and Courcoux, Salisbury; Craftsmen Potters Association.

Work represented in a number of museums and public collections in UK.

Mary Rogers

MER

Born in 1929 in Derbyshire. Lives in Cornwall. Apprenticed to a calligrapher, she trained at St Martins' School of Art and worked for many years as an illustrator. Becoming interested in clay, she set up a studio in 1960 where she experimented with modelling and building pots by hand principally in porcelain. Forms and decoration are derived from the natural world. The delicately worked porcelain is pinched, scraped, carved and sometimes pierced. The walls may be creased and overlapped like flower petals. Colour is applied to the raw clay, using a mixture of oxides painted on in pointillist fashion. Glazes are matt.

Major exhibitions include: Craftsmen Potters Association; British Crafts Centre/Contemporary Applied Arts; Oxford Gallery; Midland Gallery, Nottingham; Peter Dingley, Stratford-upon-Avon; Dartington Cider Press Gallery; Westminster Gallery, Boston; Musée des Arts Decoratifs, Lausanne; Kettles Yard, Cambridge; Graham Gallery, New York.

Work represented in many public collections in UK and overseas.

Fiona Salazar

Born in 1949 in Athens, she was educated in England and worked for the Arts Education Trust and BBC Radio Drama before studying ceramics at the Central School of Art and Design, and the Royal College of Art. She recently worked from Kingsgate Workshops in London.

Her pieces are a mixture of white earthenware and stoneware handbuilt by coiling, beaten into shape and finished off with a sponge to ensure a smooth surface. They are then sprayed with a fine slip and burnished. Decoration is applied by brush and separately burnished before firing and glazing. The final stage is wax polishing.

Major exhibitions include: British Crafts Centre/Contemporary Applied Arts; Media Gallery, London; Crafts Council at the Victoria and Albert Museum; Keramik Studio, Vienna; Contemporary Ceramics, Smiths Gallery; Crafts & Folk Art Museum, Los Angeles; Sothebys Decorative Arts Exhibition.

Work represented in a number of public collections in the UK.

Micky Schloessingk

Born in 1949 in London. Now lives in South Wales. Travelled in India in her teens where she first met with pots and pot making. A studio pottery course at Harrow was followed by workshop experience with woodfired saltglaze and earthenware in France and Spain. From 1974 she produced saltglazed tableware in a woodfired kiln in Yorkshire under the name of Micky Doherty. Moved to the Gower, South Wales in 1987. Her pots are made of a mixture of ballclays and sand, thrown and with slip applied, they are once fired in a wood firing kiln to 1310°C. Salt is introduced over a couple of hours. She is beginning to hand-build some of her pots, but they remain functional.

Major exhibitions include: Craftsmen Potters Association; Newport Museum and Art Gallery; Craft Study Centre, Bath; Castle Museum, Nottingham; Contemporary Applied Arts; The Craft Centre, and Design Gallery, Leeds; Crafts Council, Victoria and Albert Museum; Ceri Richards Gallery, Swansea.

Ray Silverman

Born in 1943 in Hertfordshire. Lives in Essex. Trained at Camberwell School of Art and Crafts and Goldsmiths' College. He spent three years in Israel designing ceramics for large scale commercial production. In 1971 he set up his studio in Hornchurch, producing mainly individual thrown pieces in stoneware and porcelain, and teaching part time at West Ham College and Goldsmiths'. The high degree of technique and finish in his studio work is a result of his industrial experience. His small forms, thrown and turned are derived from natural forms and textures. Two or three sprayed glazes produce a speckled effect graduated over the pot.

Major exhibitions include: Craftsmen Potters Association; Innate Harmony, London; Open Eye Gallery, Edinburgh; Victoria and Albert Museum, London; Paul Rice Gallery, London; British Crafts Centre, London; Galerie Munsterberg, Basle; Fitchberg Museum, Massachusetts; Galerie Schekelberg; Bonn.

Work represented in a number of public collections in the UK.

Peter Simpson

Born in 1943 in Middlesex. Lives in Hampshire. Trained at Bournemouth and Poole College of Art, initially as a sculptor. His work makes no reference to functional form. He is interested in the process of ageing, the patina of wear, and his surfaces have stamped patterns, stained, polished and worked to simulate the effect of wear through handling. He uses a porcelain clay, occasionally a white stoneware slab built, modelled or coiled, and some parts thrown. Any combination of these techniques may be used in one piece. Lastly, fine wax is applied to give a smooth patina.

Major exhibitions include: Pace Gallery, London; Bradford City Art Gallery; British Crafts Centre/Contemporary Applied Arts; Oxford Gallery; Primavera, Cambridge; International Exhibition of Ceramic Art, Tokyo; Galerie het Kapelhuis, Amersfoort, Holland; Keramion Gallery, Cologne; Galerie L, Hamburg; Gimpel Fils, London.

Work represented in many public collections in UK and overseas.

144

Richard Slee

Born in 1946 in Cumbria. Lives in Brighton. Trained at Carlisle College of Art and Design and Central School. After two years of full time teaching he set up a studio combining his own work with a busy programme of part time teaching.

He works in earthenware handbuilding and press moulding. He manipulates the clay into pinched knobbly surfaces contrasting matt and shiny, rough and smooth. Colour is important. He builds it up, glaze upon glaze. He is especially interested in the decorative ware of the industrial potteries of the eighteenth as well as the twentieth centuries.

Major exhibitions include: 'Fast Forward' – ICA and Kettles Yard, Cambridge; Bassano del Grappa, Italy; Gallery de Witte Voet, Amsterdam; Crafts Council, Victoria and Albert Museum; Dorothy Weiss Gallery, San Francisco; Contemporary Applied Arts; Gallery F 15, Oslo; East-West Contemporary Ceramics, Seoul and Hong Kong; Contemporary British Crafts, Japan.

Work is represented in a number of public collections in UK and overseas.

145

Martin Smith

Born in 1950 in Essex. Lives in London. Trained at Bristol Polytechnic and the Royal College of Art. He established his first studio in Suffolk in 1974, and moved to London in 1979. He is senior lecturer at Camberwell School of Art and Crafts.

Up to 1978 the vast majority of his work made use of the Raku process sometimes with enamel transfers for surface detailing. There followed a change to red earthenware, sometimes in a combination with other elements such as aluminium, but maintaining the vessel form. Present work uses red and white earthenwares, with the occasional use of metals and laminated brick; the process of making involves various industrial processes. An interest in functional design is leading to a number of pieces of furniture, for example tables and clocks.

Major exhibitions include: British Crafts Centre/Contemporary Applied Arts; Queensberry Hunt Studio, London; Garth Clark Gallery, New York, London; Anatol Orient, London; Crafts Council; Forms around a Vessel – travelling exhibition.

Work in many public collections in UK and overseas.

Peter Smith

Formerly a research chemist, he took evening pottery classes run by Robert Fournier. With no further formal training he went to Cornwall to make earthenware in the folk tradition, and started the Bojewyan Pottery in 1974. All his work is individual, often based on the vessel, with some sculpture. His latest work is moving toward the non-functional. He fires with a large coal burning kiln which produces a complex burning chemistry. Glazes are used only sparingly so that the body beneath is clearly visible. His 'work in clay' is unfired, and mixed with cement for strength. He likes the softness of unfired clay, and the way other materials such as metal handles can be incorporated, preserving the immediacy of the idea.

Major exhibitions include: Contemporary Applied Arts, London; Craftsmen Potters Association, London; New Craftsman, St Ives; Penwith Gallery, St Ives; Institute of Contemporary Art, London; Aberystwyth Arts Centre; Ceramics 7, Greenwich.

John Solly

Born in 1928 in Kent, lives in East Sussex. Trained at Maidstone School of Art and Central School of Art when Dora Billington was in charge of the Pottery Department. He set up his own workshop at Maidstone in 1953 and for 33 years produced domestic high fired earthenware and slipware. In 1986 he moved to Peasmarsh, and re-established his pottery in what had been a village shop. He still produces slipware and high fired earthenware by throwing and press mouldings with the emphasis on individual pieces. Since 1960 he has held an annual summer school at the Pottery. He teaches part time at Mid Kent Adult Centre.

Major exhibitions include: Craftsmen Potters Association; St James' Gallery, Bath; Ladgate Gallery, Beverley; Mastermakers, Canterbury.

Julian Stair

Born in 1955 in Bristol. Lives in London. Trained at Camberwell School
of Art and Royal College of Art. After a year at 401½ workshops and
several teaching posts he converted two derelict stables in Brixton into
four workspaces. In 1988 he took six months' break to work in the USA.
He teaches part time at Roehampton Institute of Higher Education.

Julian Stair works in porcelain and earthenware. His pieces are thrown,
decorated with oxides, painted drawn and banded, and single fired. He is
a strong believer in the value of function and practical use in pottery.

Major exhibitions include: Libertys 1988; Anton Gallery, Washington;
Crafts Council, London; Paul Rice Gallery, London; Museum fur Kunst
Und Gewerbe, Hamburg; Westminster Gallery, Boston; Anatol Orient,
London; Carmel College, Oxfordshire; Oxford Gallery; Bourne Fine Arts,
Edinburgh.

Work included in public collections in UK and overseas.

Gary Standige

Born in 1946 in Blackpool, Lancashire. Lives in Kent. Studied at Stoke-on-Trent College of Art and at the Royal College of Art under Hans Coper – a major influence on his thinking as a potter. Set up his own workshop in 1976, and now works from Aylesford in Kent at the same time as teaching ceramics at West Surrey College of Art and Design, Farnham. Major influences on his work are Cycladic Sculpture, Brancusi and crystals found during mountain climbing. He works in stoneware and porcelain, throwing on the wheel, and decorating by impressed plaster forms and by the use of fire; frequently the work is salt-fired in a variety of atmospheres and salt additions.

Major exhibitions include: Franz Zimmerman Gallery, Switzerland; Kettles Yard, Cambridge; British Crafts Centre/Contemporary Applied Arts; Craftsmen Potters Association; CPA Members, Basle, Switzerland; Victoria and Albert Museum; Southampton Art Gallery; Amalgam Barnes; Rufford Park Craft Centre.

Work included in many public and private collections.

Peter Stoodley

Born 1920 in Bournemouth. Now lives in Hampshire. Peter Stoodley trained in painting at Bournemouth and Goldsmiths' Schools of Art. He took pottery as a craft subject at Camberwell and started a pottery centre at High Barnet. He worked subsequently at Poole Pottery and began a teaching career at Bournemouth College of Art which only ended with retirement in 1980. He began making plant pots in the 1950s when pinch potting became popular and has continued ever since.

His work is unglazed vitreous slip decorated stoneware, coiled and dry thrown. His pots are made on a heavy hand turntable and decorated areas, defined by meridian lines and filled with contrasting slip.

Major exhibitions include: Suffolk Crafts Society, Aldeburgh; Victoria and Albert Museum; Terrace Gallery, Worthing; Craftsmen Potters Association; Bohun Gallery, Henley-on-Thames; Oxford Gallery.

Angus Suttie

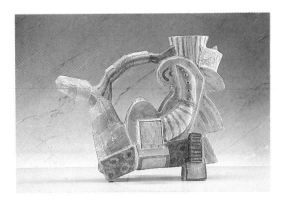

Born in 1946 in Myreton, Scotland. Living in London. Studied a Camberwell School of Arts and Crafts where he now teaches in the Foundation Department. Angus Suttie is heavily influenced by artists such as Miro, Klee, Picasso and Kandinsky, and is in love with South American pottery.

He works in red earthenware clay fired to 1140°C for the first glaze firing and subsequently to 1040°C. The methods of marking and decorating are improvised. His most recent work is still based loosely on the vessel form, but more hard edged and geometric than earlier work and with muted colours.

Major exhibitions include: Crafts Council Gallery; The Orchard Gallery, Londonderry; The Power House Museum, Sydney; Anatol Orient, London; Victoria and Albert Museum; 1987 British Council tour of South America.

Geoffrey Swindell

Born in 1945 in Stoke-on-Trent. Now lives in Cardiff. Studied at Stoke-on-Trent College of Art and Royal College of Art from 1967 to 1970. Now full time lecturer at South Glamorgan Institute of Higher Education, Cardiff.

The sculptural and formal tradition of Ruth Duckworth, Lucie Rie and Hans Coper has been a strong influence. His vessel forms are porcelain, small and precisely structured. Various surface qualities are achieved with lustres blended or sprayed with paraffin to create mottled effects. Some pots are sand-blasted to give a delicate pitted surface. This often results in breakages. The finishing process is lengthy.

Geoffrey Swindell makes pots only in the winter months. Most of his work is sold in the USA and West Germany.

Major exhibitions include: British Craft Centre; Oxford Gallery; National Museum of Wales; Graham Gallery, New York; Beaux Arts, Bath.

Work represented in many museums and public collections worldwide.

153

Sutton Taylor

Born in 1943 in Yorkshire. Lives in Leeds. Self taught, he has worked from a pottery in Kingston, Jamaica (1966–70), and from three potteries in Leeds since then. He has also taught in Manchester and Jamaica.

He works in high fired earthenware and porcelain. His pieces are usually large thrown bowls which he looks upon as canvases for painting with the pigment lustre technique. Lustres are formed by fusing on to the already fired glaze surface a fine film of metal. The gases from a wood burning kiln enhance the process, and the uncertainties.

Major exhibitions include: Oxford Gallery; Westminster Gallery, Boston; Leeds City Art Gallery; Copernican Connection, Yorkshire; Queensberry Hunt Studio, London; Sheila Harrison Fine Art; Keramion Museum, Frechen; Vallauris Biennale, France; Gainsborough House, Sudbury.

Work represented in public collections in UK and overseas.

Janice Tchalenko

Born in 1942 in Rugby. Lives in London. Trained at Harrow College of Art before setting up her workshop in 1971, in South London. She teaches part time at the Royal College of Art. She was commissioned as a design consultant for a range of very successful tableware produced by Dart Pottery and has also designed for Designers Guild and Next Interiors. In 1988 she won the Radio 4/Radio Times Enterprise Award for Small Businesses for her work with Dart Pottery.

Her own pieces are high fired reduced stoneware, thrown and press moulded and decorated unfired with bright coloured glazes trailed and painted.

Major exhibitions include: Crafts Council; New Ashgate Gallery, Farnham; Bohun Gallery, Henley-on-Thames; Westminster Gallery, Boston; Blumhelman Gallery, New York; Serpentine Gallery, London; Contemporary British Crafts, Kyoto/Tokyo; Galerie Charlotte Hennig, Darmstadt.

Work included in a number of public collections in UK and overseas.

James Tower

1919-1988. A painting student at the Royal Academy and the Slade School, and a lover of traditional English pottery, he trained in ceramics at the Central School under Dora Billington. His pottery developed during his years teaching at Bath Academy of Art. He became Head of Sculpture at Brighton College of Art in 1965, retiring in 1986. During the 1960s and 1970s, James Tower produced large terracotta pieces. Towards the end of the 1970s he moved towards large glazed 'forms to paint on' mainly moulded and reminiscent of water and marine forms. Decoration involved three, four or five firings. Over a white tin glaze a darker glaze was added, which when dry was partially removed with the fingers. The relationship between decoration and form was always of paramount importance to James Tower.

Major exhibitions include: Rotterdam and USA, 1960; Arts Council; Worthing Art Gallery; Gimpel Fils, London; Gardener Centre, Sussex University; Art Latitude, New York; Gallery 99, Miami; Sheila Harrison Fine Art, London.

Marianne de Trey

Born in London in 1913. Lives at Dartington, Devon. Trained at the Royal College of Art as a textile designer. Married the potter TS Haile and began to learn about pottery in the United States during the war. In 1947 they moved to Dartington to take over the workshop at Shinners Bridge. TS Haile was killed in an accident shortly afterwards. Marianne de Trey's was one of the first post-war workshops selling tableware and providing workshop experience. In the early years she worked in earthenware. She has now phased out the domestic ware and works alone on individual pieces, mostly in porcelain. They are hand thrown, and decorated with wax resist, sgraffito and coloured slips. They reflect her interest in pattern, derived from natural forms and textiles.

Major exhibitions include: Craftsmen Potters Association; Primavera, London, Cambridge; Cider Press Centre, Dartington; Kettles Yard, Cambridge; Boymans Museum, Rotterdam; English Gallery, Boston; English Gallery, Geisenheim; Galleries in Chagford, Exmouth, Exeter and other centres in the South West.

Judy Trim

Born in 1943 in Cambridge. Lives in London. Trained as an Art Teacher at Bath Academy of Art 1961–64. Studied pottery under James Tower. Taught Art and Craft in London schools for many years and only began to develop her own work about 1978 with her first exhibition in 1980. Visiting lecturer at a number of Art schools. She works slowly, evolving each pot from the previous one and referring to the classical Cycladic, Indian and Egyptian traditions. She particularly admires the work of Hans Coper, Lucie Rie and Elizabeth Fritsch.

She works in red earthenware and stoneware, coiling and decorating in a variety of ways, including burnishing or spraying in coloured slips, carving, sgraffito, smoking and precious metal lustres.

Major exhibitions include: Craftsmen Potters Association; Oxford Gallery; Bluecoate Display Centre, Liverpool; Atmosphere, London; Contemporary Applied Arts, London; Westminster Gallery, Boston; Anatol Orient, London; Sheila Harrison Fine Art, London; Crafts Council.

Work represented in a number of public collections in the UK and overseas.

Sidney Tustin

Born in 1914 at Winchcombe. At the age of thirteen he began work at the reopened Winchcombe pottery, initially turning the wheel for Elijah Comfort, the chief thrower employed at Winchcombe before its closure. In 1929 Sidney Tustin began a three year apprenticeship and continued to work for Michael Cardew until his departure for Wenford Bridge in 1939. Sindey's brother Charles joined the pottery in 1935, and both brothers were conscripted into the army until 1946 when Sidney returned to Winchcombe. He made jugs, porridge bowls, soup bowls, butter coolers, and jam pots – most kinds of domestic ware apart from large pots.

He retired in 1978 having made over a million pots in fifty-one years at Winchcombe.

Angela Verdon

Born in 1949 in Derby. Still lives in Derbyshire. Studied ceramics at Wolverhampton Polytechnic and the Royal College of Art. Combined part-time lecturing at Worthing College with working for industry at Moira Pottery in Leicestershire. During a craft fellowship year at Gladstone Pottery Museum she started to experiment with bone china, a medium in which she has worked ever since.

Her pieces are mainly cast with a little press moulding, and pierced at a low bisque stage, then refired and hand burnished. Work is developing with the use of staining by means of oxides and the introduction of precious metals inlaid into the clay.

Major exhibitions include: Oxford Gallery; New Ashgate Gallery, Farnham; Graham Gallery, New York; Westminster Gallery, Boston; Craftsmen Potters Association; Scottish Gallery, Edinburgh, Godfrey and Twatt, Harrogate, Galerie L, Hamburg; Bohun Gallery, Henley-on-Thames.

Alan Wallwork

Born in 1931 in Hertfordshire. Lives in Dorset. After a brief period at Goldsmiths' College and two workshops in London, he moved to Dorset in 1964. Working with assistants, he produced a wide range of stoneware and earthenware, garden pots, sculptural pieces, etc, and exhibited widely in the UK and overseas. In the 1970s he exhibited infrequently, concentrating on tile production, but in 1984 moved to his present workshop overlooking Lyme Bay where he makes hand-built stoneware and porcelain. He is especially concerned with the tactile qualities of ceramic forms and surfaces and is much influenced by natural forms. Pieces are coiled, pinched or slabbed, often coated with clays of different compositions and materials which will leave cavities and textured surfaces when fired.

He dislikes the concept of working specifically for exhibitions. His work can be bought from the Craftsmen Potters Association, and JK Hill, London.

John Ward

Born in 1938 in London. Lives in Wales. Studied ceramics at Camberwell School of Art and Crafts. He set up his first workshop in 1970 and taught part time until 1979 when he moved to Wales to pot full time.

He uses his own recipe of clay mixed by hand. All his work is hand-built by coiling clay to form hollow vessels, sometimes cut and rejoined to create ridges and grooves, and finally scraped and partly burnished with a pebble. Each pot is twice fired. Glazes are poured, sprayed and painted sometimes with painted decoration beneath. His main preoccupation is the development of simple hollow forms; function is secondary to form.

Major exhibitions include: Peter Dingley, Stratford-upon-Avon; Craftsmen Potters Association, London; Amalgam, Barnes; Beaux Arts, Bath; Contemporary Applied Arts; Crafts Council, Victoria and Albert Museum; Galerie Gilbert, Remetschweil, Germany.

162

Sasha Wardell

Born in 1956 in Negombo, Sri Lanka. Now lives in Wiltshire. Trained at Bath Academy of Art and North Staffordshire Polytechnic, Stoke-on-Trent. Since 1981 has had a busy teaching programme. Now lectures part time at Bath College of Higher Education (Bath Academy). Her work is slip cast bone china. The models are turned on a plaster lathe then carved to introduce twists and facets. After moulding they are cast very thinly to enhance translucency, then fired to 1260°C. Decoration is applied by airbrush through a series of masks, and the piece is fired for a second time. Finally it is polished by hand to achieve an egg-shell matt finish.

Major exhibitions include: Bohun Gallery, Henley-on-Thames; Beaux Arts, Bath; New Craftsman Gallery, St Ives; Amalgam, Barnes; Oxford Gallery; Scottish Gallery; New Ashgate Gallery, Farnham; Keramic Studio, Vienna; L A Craft Museum.

Robert Johnson Washington

Born in 1913 in London. Living in Essex. After training in painting at Goldsmiths' and the Royal College of Art in the 1930s he first saw the work of William Straite Murray and stayed on at the Royal College of Art for a further year to study ceramics. Strongly influenced by Straite Murray and also by Dora Billington he has produced pots sporadically over the years while teaching. They have been stoneware with figurative decoration reminiscent of Sam Haile. He is now potting full time and re-examining earlier principles, trying to evolve a synthesis between ceramics and painting.

RJ Washington's present pieces combine throwing and slabbing and are often fired four or five times. He may use fibreglass, metal or glass in the decoration.

Recent exhibitions at: Anatol Orient; Paul Rice Gallery. Works exhibited by: Victoria and Albert Museum; Fitzwilliam Museum, Cambridge; Cleveland, Paisley, Hertford Museums.

Jason Wason

Born in 1946 in Liverpool. Now lives and works in an isolated farmhouse on the moors about St Just, Cornwall. Travelled for six years in Europe, Africa and India before forming a crafts cooperative in Scotland in 1972. From 1976 to 1981 he worked with Bernard and Janet Leach at the Leach Pottery, St Ives.

He works in raku which he finds appealing for its dramatic technique. All manner of metallic lustrous surfaces are revealed, contrasting with the scorched, blackened clay body. The piece illustrated is from his 'excavation' series.

Major exhibitions include: New Craftsman, St Ives; Penwith Gallery, St Ives; Beaux Arts, Bath; Amalgam, Barnes; Austin Desmond Gallery, London; Leeds City Art Gallery; Bradford City Art Gallery; Frankfurt Museum.

Represented in private collections in USA, Germany and Japan.

165

Robin Welch

Born in 1936 in Warwickshire. Now lives in Suffolk. Trained at th
Central School of Art and started his own workshop in London in 196(
Moved to Australia in 1962 to establish a pottery worshop, returning i
1965 to settle in Suffolk. He has lectured extensively at home an
overseas, including a period as artist in residence at Indiana University.

He works in stoneware, building up shapes on to thrown bases with
rolled slabs of clay loosely built and joined. The surface textures an
colours often require many firings at different temperatures. Glazes an
colour, enamels and lustres may be added one over another.

Major exhibitions include: Oxford Gallery; International Exhibition
Milan; Kettles Yard, Cambridge; Beaux Arts, Bath; Craftsmen Potter
Association; JK Hill, London; Henley Museum, Stoke-on-Trent; Galeri
An Gross St Martin, Cologne.

Work exhibited in many public and private collections.

166

Reginald Wells

1877–1951. Trained at Camberwell School of Art, he was a sculptor who turned to pottery in about 1909. He worked at Coldrum near Wrotham in Kent, making brown glazed earthenware, sometimes decorated with white slip. He was the first artist potter to turn to English traditions for his inspiration. He moved to Chelsea, and in 1925 to Storrington in Sussex where he began to produce stoneware in the Chinese style with thick glazes sometimes crackled.

Examples of his work can be seen in the Victoria and Albert Museum.

Geoffrey Whiting

1919–1988. Born in the Midlands and trained as an architect. During war service in India he worked with a family of village potters. Returning home, he gave up architecture and started Avoncraft Pottery in Worcestershire building a coal and woodfired kiln and making first slipware then stoneware. In 1955 he moved to Droitwich, continuing to make stoneware and some porcelain domesticware. In 1972 he set up a workshop in Canterbury combining pottery with some teaching. Best known for his teapots which Bernard Leach described as among the best ever made. He held few exhibitions and never made pots especially for such occasions, preferring to put aside a few suitable pieces from normal production to sell though the Craftsmen Potters Association, and a handful of provincial outlets.

His work is represented in a number of public collections in the UK and overseas.

Kate Wickham

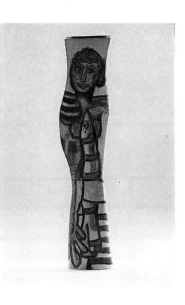

Born in 1953 in Sheffield. Now lives and works in London. Trained at Rochdale College of Art, Camberwell School of Art, and the Royal College of Art. She teaches part time on a foundation course ceramics, drawing and sculpture.

Her work is white stoneware fired to 1140°C. All pieces are hand-built, using slab building and coiling techniques. They are painted with under glaze colours and oxides, and once fired. No glazes are used.

Major exhibitions include: Amalgam, Barnes; Anatol Orient; Oriel 31 Gallery, Welshpool; Curwen Gallery, Dublin; Westminster Gallery, Boston; Galerie fur Englishche Keramik, Heidelberg; Artsite, Bath.

Mary Wondrausch

Born in 1923 in London. Now living near Guildford, Surrey. A part time pottery student at Farnham School of Art, Mary Wondrausch only took up pottery full time when her family had grown up. Her greatest pleasure is in working to commission rather than for exhibition. Her inspiration comes from Folk Art and the word itself plays a major role in her craft, conveying both sentiment and humour. She works in earthenware, decorating in either the slip-trailed or sgraffito manner under a honey or clear glaze. In 1986 she published *Mary Wondrausch on Slipware.*

Major exhibitions include: Alton Museum; British Craft Centre/ Contemporary Applied Arts; Amalgam, Barnes; Craftsmen Potters Association; Primavera, Cambridge; City Museum, Stoke-on-Trent.

Gary Wornell

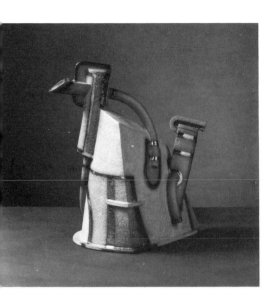

Born in 1952 in Montreal. Now living in Suffolk. Trained at Lowestoft School of Art and Stoke-on-Trent, before setting up his present studio. Lectures part time at Lowestoft College of Art, Croydon College and University of East Anglia School of Education.

His early work was oriental influenced porcelain, predominantly thrown, though including inlay, porcelain jewellery, and various exploratory stages such as raku. More recently he has switched to working entirely in terra cotta, throwing or hand-building with burnished slips and selected areas of glaze and lustre. The scale of his work is becoming larger, and he now uses a computer to make final adjustments to the electric firing process.

Major exhibitions include: Libertys, One Off; Buro Ledeboer, The Hague, Holland; Rufford Arts Centre; Westminster Gallery, Boston; Anatol Orient, London; Norwich Castle; Craftsmen Potters Association.

Denise Wren

1891–1979. Born in Western Australia, she studied as a design student at Kingston-on-Thames School of Art (1907–12) under Archibald Knox, and there she began to experiment with pottery, teaching herself to throw. She started a pottery in Kingston in 1911 which she transferred to Oxshott, Surrey where she and her husband built a house and pottery workshops. Here she designed a series of small cokefired kilns and made the plans available to other potters at a time when there was little technical information available. He work before the war was earthenware with coloured glazes; after the war, stoneware and saltglazed pots and later the many modelled elephants. Together with her husband she wrote books on pottery and ran short courses at Oxshott, and did much to bring pottery to the attention of the public.

Her work was exhibited at the British Empire Exhibitions 1923–24, at the Commonwealth Institute, and, with her daughter, Rosemary, at Berkeley Galleries in the 1960s. It is represented in a number of public collections in the UK including the Victoria and Albert Museum.

Rosemary Wren and Peter Crotty

Rosemary Wren born in 1922 at Oxshott, Surrey; Peter Crotty in 1943 in Essex. Rosemary, the daughter of Denise and Henry Wren, trained at Guildford School of Art under Willi Soukop and Helen Pincombe, and the Royal College of Art. In 1950 she set up her own workshop under the Oxshott Pottery umbrella, and was subsequently shown the method of making animal and bird forms by Francine Delpierre and Albert Diato. In 1970 she teamed up with Peter Crotty and in 1978 they moved from Oxshott to Devon.

Peter Crotty had a background of gouache painting before being introduced to pottery. He took over kiln firing and now decorates pieces made by Rosemary. Each is derived from a drawing and begins with a stoneware bowl shape on to which are layered shaped strips of clay. Patterns are incised and decorated in shiny and matt glazes.

Major exhibitions include: Burlington Arcade, with Denise K Wren; Prague International 1962; Craftsmen Potters Association; International Ceramics, Victoria and Albert Museum; Casson Gallery, London; Cider Press, Dartington; Aberystwyth Arts Centre.

Takeshi Yasuda

Signature on paper label

Born in 1943 in Tokyo. Lives in Devon. He trained at the Daisei-Gama Pottery at Mashiko, Japan, and subsequently established his own workshop there. Came to the UK to work in 1973. Since then he has been craftsman in residence in Bergen, Norway and Potter in residence at Cleveland Crafts Centre, Middlesborough. Teaches from time to time at West Surrey College of Art and Design.

His pieces are thrown functional stoneware, stemming from the Japanese country tradition, decorated with slips, coloured glazes and stamped patterns.

Major exhibitions include: Crafts Council; Beaux Arts, Bath; New Ashgate Gallery, Farnham; Contemporary Applied Arts, London; Cleveland Crafts Centre, Middlesbrough; British Potters, Sandhausen, Germany; Galerie de Vier Linden, Holland; Gainsborough House, Sudbury; Made in Britain, Berlin; Crawford College of Art and Design, Cork; Godfrey and Twatt, Harrogate.

Work included in public collections in UK and overseas.

Poh Chap Yeap

Born in 1927 in Malaysia. Lives in Surrey. Began potting in Denmark before studying at Hammersmith College of Art and the Royal College of Art under Lord Queensberry. He set up the pottery department at St Paul's School, London, and taught at Hammersmith and Brighton Polytechnics. His work is wheel thrown porcelain and stoneware, bowls, dishes and bottles in the Chinese tradition. His glazes are crackled, celadons, yellows and reds.

Major exhibitions include: Ashmolean Museum, Oxford; Grosvenor Gallery, London; Casson Gallery, London; Somers Gallery, Heidelberg; Mitsukoshi Store, Tokyo; International Contemporary Ceramics, Faenza; Crafts Council, Victoria and Albert Museum, London; Graham Gallery, New York; The Reid Gallery, Guildford.

Works represented in a number of public collections in UK and overseas.

Andrew and Joanna Young   A & J YOUNG

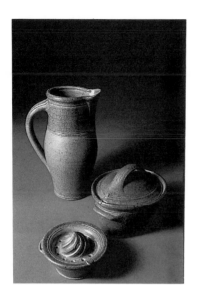

Born in 1949 and 1950 in Cambridge and Farnham respectively. They met on the Ceramics Degree Course at West Surrey College of Art, Farnham. They set up a joint workshop in 1975 in Norfolk to make a range of practical domestic stoneware pots, having been influenced by the stoneware made at La Borne in France, where they had worked for a short while with Gwyn Hanssen. Their present range of ware has been produced for the last seven years. They plan to introduce some changes with the help of a bursary. Several of their designs are being thrown in Stoke-on-Trent for Next Interiors.

Major exhibitions include: Gainsborough House, Sudbury; Victoria and Albert Museum – CPA; British Crafts Centre/Contemporary Applied Arts; New Ashgate Gallery, Farnham; Crafts Council; Craftsmen Potters Association.

Monica Young

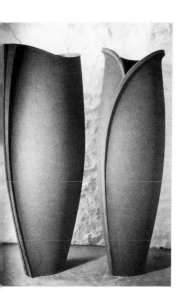

Born 1929 in Paris. Now living in North Yorkshire. Studied painting at Ealing School of Art and at the Escuella de Bellas Artes in Barcelona. Practised as a painter and book illustrator in England and Spain until 1972 when she began to teach herself to coil pots. Established a permanent workshop in North Yorkshire in 1973.

Monica Young's work is stoneware clay fired to 1300°C. Her pots are either traditional shapes or abstract forms, coil built and large, often 5 feet high, as are those illustrated. Her pots are unglazed but fired to a dark toasted colour.

Major exhibitions include: British Craft Centre; Oxford Gallery; Copernican Connection, Beverley; Scottish Gallery; Candover Gallery; Gainsborough House, Sudbury; Hannah Peschar Gallery, Ockley.

Galleries Selling Contemporary Ceramics

LONDON

Amalgam Art
3 Barnes High Street
SW13 9LB
Tel. 01 878 1279

10am–1.30pm, 2.30pm–6pm Tuesday–Saturday
Six annual exhibitions, specializing in container forms rather than
sculptural work from a range of well established and young potters.
Predominantly stoneware and earthenware, but some porcelain.

Galerie Besson
15 Royal Arcade
28 Old Bond Street
W1X 3HD
Tel. 01 491 1706

10am–5.30pm Tuesday–Friday, 10am–12.30pm Saturday
Ten annual exhibitions selling the work of established and promising
young potters, together with major modern potters such as Hans Coper,
Lucie Rie, Bernard Leach, Michael Cardew.

Cecilia Colman Gallery
67 St Johns Wood High Street
NW8 7N1
Tel. 01 722 0686

10am–5.30pm Monday–Friday, 2–5pm Saturdays
Six to eight annual exhibitions, selling sculptural and decorative one-off
pieces by contemporary potters.

Contemporary Applied Arts
43 Earlham Street, Covent Garden
WC2 9LD
Tel. 01 836 6993

10am–5.30pm Monday–Saturday
Approximately five ceramics exhibitions annually. CAA is a membership
association and exhibits a wide range of works by crafts people from the
UK and abroad. As well as exhibitions, the basement shop regularly
stocks studio and domestic ceramics.

178

Crafts Council Shop
Victoria and Albert Museum
SW7 2RL
Tel. 01 589 5070

10am–5.30pm Monday–Saturday, Sunday 2.30–5.30pm
Ten annual exhibitions by contemporary craftsmen, including domestic
pottery and sculptural ceramics. Work selected from makers on the Crafts
Council Index, recipients of Crafts Council setting-up grants, or
represented in the Crafts Council collection.

Craftsmen Potters Association
7 Marshall Street
W1V 1FD
Tel. 01 437 7605

10am–5.30pm Monday–Saturday, until 7pm on Thursdays
About 12 annual exhibitions. The CPA is a retail outlet promoting and
selling work produced by over 150 members. It sells only studio pots,
both one-off pieces and domestic ware. Work by a wide range of
members is always available.

Sheila Harrison Fine Art
121 Jermyn Street
SW1Y 4UG
Tel. 01 321 0366

10am–6pm Monday–Friday 10am–4pm Saturdays
Between six and eight annual exhibitions. Work sold includes both
contemporary and major modern potters such as Coper, Bernard Leach
and Hamada.

Michaelson & Orient
318 Portobello Road
W10 5RU
Tel. 01 969 4119

10.30am–5.30pm Tuesday–Saturday
Eleven annual exhibitions in the gallery plus various contemporary art
fairs. As well as solo exhibitions of contemporary potters, mixed work too
is always on show.

REGIONAL GALLERIES

Avon

Beaux Arts
York Street
Bath
Tel. 0225 64850

10am–6pm Monday–Saturday
Seven annual exhibitions selling work by both established and promising contemporary potters. Work by major modern potters such as Hans Coper, Lucie Rie, Bernard Leach and Michael Cardew is also stocked.

Cornwall

New Craftsman
24 Fore Street
St Ives TR26 1HE
Tel. 0736 795652

Summer 10am–6pm Monday–Saturday, 2pm–6pm Sunday
Winter 10am–5pm Monday–Saturday
No specific exhibitions but work of contemporary potters and Bernard Leach and the Leach Pottery regularly on show.

Gloucestershire

The Chestnut Gallery
High Street
Bourton-on-the-Water
Cheltenham GL54 2AN
Tel. 0451 20017

10am–5pm Monday–Saturday
11.30am–5pm Sundays and holidays
Closed Mondays, Wednesdays November–May
Two annual exhibitions. The gallery shows the work of about fifty contemporary potters towards the 'traditional' end of the market.

Hampshire

The Candover Gallery
22 West Street
Alresford SO24 9AE
Tel. 096273 3200

9.30am–5.30pm Monday-Saturday
Three annual exhibitions of contemporary potters.

Nottinghamshire

Rufford Craft Centre
Rufford Country Park
Nr Ollerton, Newark
Tel. 0636 822944

10.30am–5pm daily
Six major gallery exhibitions. Three major outdoor sculpture shows
annually. Regular shows of established and new potters' work.

Oxfordshire

Oxford Gallery
23 High Street
Oxford OX1 4AH
Tel. 0865 242731

10am–1pm, 1.30pm–5pm Monday-Saturday
Eleven annual exhibitions of work by contemporary potters.

Surrey

New Ashgate Gallery
Wagon Yard Car Park
Downing Street
Farnham GU9 7JR
Tel. 0252 713208

10am–1.30pm, 2.30pm–5pm Tuesday-Saturday
Ten annual exhibitions in the main gallery, and an adjoining craft gallery
with work by a wide range of contemporary potters. In addition to
exhibiting work by established artists, the gallery promotes young
promising potters.

Sussex

Hugo Barclay
7 East Street
Brighton BN1 1HP
Tel. 0273 21694

10am–1pm, 2pm–5.30pm Monday–Saturday
About four major exhibitions annually. Some one- or two-person shows.
Some group shows. An extensive range of established and up and coming
craftsmen, and functional and decorative works.

Warwickshire

Peter Dingley Gallery
8 Chapel Street
Stratford Upon Avon CV37 3EP
Tel. 0789 205001

9.30am–1.30pm, 2.30pm–5.30pm Monday–Saturday.
Closed Thursday pm
About five annual exhibitions, showing work from well known and less
well known potters from all over the country. One-person exhibitions are
held in spring and autumn, and work from about 10 potters is collected
in a summer show.

Wiltshire

Courcoux and Courcoux Contemporary Art
90/92 Crane Street
Salisbury SP1 2QD
Tel. 0722 333471

10am–5pm Tuesday–Saturday
Two focal exhibitions annually. Work by leading ceramicists always on
show including contemporary potters and Hans Coper, Bernard Leach,
Michael Cardew.

Yorkshire

Copernican Connection
Church Farm
Garton-on-the-Wolds
Nr Driffield
Tel. 0377 43988

10am–5pm Wednesday–Sunday
About six annual exhibitions including work by contemporary potters.

Godfrey & Twatt
7 Westminster Arcade
Parliament Street
Harrogate HG1 2RN
Tel. 0423 525300

10am–5.30pm Monday–Saturday
Four annual exhibitions. The gallery stocks a selection of domestic and studio ceramics by contemporary potters.

The Ladygate Gallery
1 Ladygate
Beverley HU17 8BH
Tel. 0482 869715

10am–5pm Monday–Saturday. Closed Thursday.
Two annual exhibitions. The gallery sells one-off pieces concentrating on figurative and decorative work and form.

Scotland

The Scottish Gallery
94 George Street
Edinburgh EH2 3DF
Tel. 031 225 5955

10am–6pm Monday–Friday, 10am–1pm Saturday
Monthly exhibitions: either solus or theme shows. Domestic and individual works, established and young potters.

Wales

Oriel 31
31 High Street
Welshpool
Powys SY21 7JP
Tel. 0938 2990

11am–5pm Monday–Saturday
About ten annual exhibitions showing work of a wide range of contemporary potters. There are no particular potters whose work is stocked on a regular basis.

183

Oriel 31
Davies Memorial Gallery
The Park
Newtown
Powys SY16 2NZ
Tel. 0686 25041

10am–5pm Monday-Saturday
Eight annual exhibitions of contemporary ceramics, both sculptural and functional domestic ware. An artist's work is rarely shown more than once.

Auctions

Two London auction houses specialize in studio ceramics. Each has about three auctions a year at which work by a wide range of modern potters is sold.

Bonhams
Montpelier Galleries
Montpelier Street
Knightsbridge
SW7 1HN
Tel. 01 584 9161

and

Christie Manson & Woods
Decorative Arts Department
8 King Street
St James's
SW1Y 6QT
Tel. 01 839 9060

Collections

A number of museums throughout Britain have permanent collections of modern pottery. The following are some of those worth visiting:

Aberystwyth

Aberystwyth Arts Centre
University College of Wales
Penglais Hill

Bath

Crafts Study Centre
Holburne Museum
Great Pulteney Street

Cambridge

Fitzwilliam Museum
Trumpington Street

Leeds

Lotherton Hall
Aberford
Nr Leeds

Leicester

Leicester Museum & Art Gallery
New Walk

London

Victoria & Albert Museum
Cromwell Road, SW7

Norwich

Sainsbury Centre for Visual Arts
University of East Anglia

Southampton

Southampton City Art Gallery
Civic Centre

Sudbury

Sudbury Hall
Sudbury
Derbyshire

York

York City Art Gallery
Exhibition Square

Bibliography

Birks, Tony, *Art of the Modern Potter*, Country Life Books, 1976

Birks, Tony, *Hans Coper*, Collins, 1983

Birks, Tony, *Lucie Rie*, A & C Black, 1987

Cameron, Elisabeth and Philippa Lewis, *Potters on Pottery*, Evans Bros, 1976

Michael Cardew, Crafts Advisory Committee, 1976

Casson, Michael, *Pottery in Britain Today*, Tiranti, 1967

Clark, Garth, *Michael Cardew*, Faber, 1978

Cooper, Ronald, G, *The Modern Potter*, Tiranti, 1947

Digby, George Winfield, *The Work of the Modern Potter in England*, John Murray, 1952

Dormer, Peter, *The New Ceramics*, Thames & Hudson, 1986

Dormer, Peter and David Cripps, *Elizabeth Fritsch in Studio*, Bellew, 1985

Dormer, Peter and David Cripps, *Alison Britton in Studio*, Bellew, 1985

Haslam, Malcolm, *William Staite Murray*, Crafts Council, 1984

Hogben, Carol, *The Art of Bernard Leach*, Faber, 1978

Houston, John and David Cripps, *Lucie Rie*, Crafts Council, 1981

Lane, Peter, *Studio Ceramics*, Collins, 1983

Lane, Peter, *Ceramic Form*, Collins, 1988

Leach, Bernard, *Bernard Leach*, Asahi Shimbun, Tokyo, 1966

Leach, Bernard, *A Potter's Book*, Faber, 1945

Leach, Bernard, *A Potters Work*, Adams & Dart, 1967

Katharine Pleydell-Bouverie: 1895–1985, *A Potter's Life*, Crafts Council, 1986

Rose, Muriel, *Artist Potters in England*, Faber, 1970

187

GALERIE BESSON

Founded in 1988, Galerie Besson is London's leading gallery to specialize in the work of contemporary and modern studio potters. It holds regular exhibitions of work by potters from Britain and abroad and has an extensive stock of pots by HANS COPER, LUCIE RIE, BERNARD LEACH, MICHAEL CARDEW and KATHARINE PLEYDELL-BOUVERIE, and by the foremost potters of the next generation, including EWEN HENDERSON, ELIZABETH FRITSCH, IAN GODFREY, ELIZABETH RAEBURN, GUTTE ERIKSEN, CLAUDI CASANOVAS and VLADIMIR TSIVIN.

Lucie Rie: Porcelain bowl, 1955, diam: 19.1 cm

15 ROYAL ARCADE   28 OLD BOND STREET
LONDON W1X 3HD   01-491 1706   *FAX:* 01-495 3203

Tuesday–Friday 10–5.30   Saturday 10–12.30   Monday by appointment

BEAUX ARTS CERAMICS

York Street, Bath   Tel. (0225) 464850

Regular exhibitions of leading 20th Century potters

open 10-5 Mon.-Sat.

Illustrated: Magdalene Oduno. Handbuilt Burnished and Polished Black Earthenware Vase

amalgam

3 Barnes High Street, London SW13 9LB

Open: Tuesday - Saturday
10 - 1.30 and 2.30 - 6pm

Telephone: (01) 878 1279

Stock and Exhibit Ceramics by:

Molly Attrill
Svend Bayer
Sebastian Blackie
Sandy Brown
James Campbell
Daphne Carnegy
Trevor Corser
Nigel Cox
Mike Dodd
Carolyn Elieu
Ewen Henderson
Paul Jackson
Colin Kellam
Anna Lambert
Janet Leach

John Maltby
Jon Middlemiss
Colin Pearson
Richard Phethern
Deborah Prosser
Anthony Phillips
C.A. Richards
Rupert Spira
Jason Shackleton
John Ward
David White
Karen Wood
Pam Wright
Peter Wright

Stocks are subject to availability. This list is not exhaustive. We also exhibit original prints, watercolours, blown glass and studio jewellery.

CECILIA COLMAN GALLERY
67 St Johns Wood High Street NW8 7NL
01 722 0686

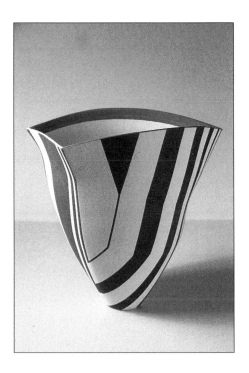

One of London's most established galleries,
representing contemporary studio potters.
We exhibit a comprehensive collection of
works in clay, with a fresh, innovative
approach.

a Crafts Council selected gallery
a Member of the Independent Craft Galleries Association

NEW ASHGATE GALLERY

FINE AND APPLIED ARTS

CERAMICS

Wagon Yard • Farnham • Surrey • (0252) 713208

An Illustrated Dictionary of British Steel Engravers

Basil Hunnisett

First published in 1980, Dr Hunnisett's *Dictionary of British Steel Engravers* was the first book to assemble in a single volume the entire corpus of the British engraver of the 19th century. Since it is the engraver who makes the plate from which the finished product is taken, his is the art which fashioned it, and the artistic ability of such men mostly equalled that of the artist employed to produce the original drawings. Yet little or nothing is known of them. This new and completely revised edition includes a substantial plate section, thus providing a chronological dimension to the volume as well as illustrating the art of steel engraving in its various phases.

224 pages   Hbk   0 85967 740 0   £37.50

The Criers and Hawkers of London: Engravings and Drawings by Marcellus Laroon

Edited by Sean Shesgreen

Published in 1687 and a best-seller the day it appeared, the present volume includes plates from the 1760 edition in which designs were updated to provide us with a unique comparison of the changes in art and working life between 1687 and the late eighteenth century. The book also contains nineteen hitherto unpublished sketches by Laroon held at Blenheim Palace - seven of which were never engraved.

270 pages   Hbk   0 85967 811 3   £45.00

Benjamin Fawcett: Printer and Engraver

Edited by Ruari McLean

Benjamin Fawcett (1808-1893) was the outstanding English woodblock colour printer of the nineteenth century. This beautiful volume includes previously unpublished illustrations, essays on Fawcett's life, popular scientific publishing in the nineteenth century and Fawcett's colour wood-block techniques, and a checklist of all known publications containing plates by Fawcett, with every individual plate listed.

200 pages   Hbk   0 8596 7789 3   £47.50

Early Christian Art and Architecture

Robert Milburn

This readable and attractive book provides a wide-ranging account of all aspects of artistic and architectural achievement in the Christian world up to the middle of the sixth century. Excavation in recent decades has unearthed a remarkable collection of sites and objects which illustrate the growth of the Christian Church and its way of life. The classic achievements of Rome, Ravenna and Constantinople are of course included, but so are discoveries in outposts of Syria, the Balkans and North Africa. With photographs, plans and maps the whole field of early Christian art and architecture is surveyed.

336 pages, over 200 illustrations
Hbk   0 85967 634 X   £35.00

The Camden Town Group

Wendy Baron

408 pages, 156 plates, 8 in colour
Hbk   0 85967 517 3   £55.00

The Euston Road School

A Study in Objective Painting

Bruce Laughton

404 pages, 218 illustrations and 17 colour plates   Hbk   0 85967 694 3   £48.50

Pietro Testa 1612-1650

Prints and Drawings

Elizabeth Cropper

428 pages, 269 illustrations
Hbk   0 85967 802 4   £35.00

Gwen John

Mary Taubman

136 pages, including 28 colour and 56 monochrome plates
Hbk   0 85967 694 3   £25.00

Edward Bawden: War Artist

Edited by Ruari McLean

Foreword by Edward Bawden

96 pages, over 40 illustrations, 24 in colour
Hbk   0 85967 695 1   £19.50

Scolar Press

—— Scolar Press, Gower House, Croft Road, Aldershot, ——
Hampshire, GU11 3HR   Tel. No. (0252) 331551